University of Sheffield
LGBT Library

Please return this item by the date below

Portraits to the Wall

A new series of books from Cassell's Sexual Politics list,
Women on Women *provides a forum for lesbian, bisexual
and heterosexual women to explore and debate
contemporary issues and to develop strategies for the
advancement of feminist culture and politics into the next
century*

COMMISSIONING:
Roz Hopkins
Liz Gibbs
Christina Ruse

Portraits to the Wall

Historic Lesbian Lives Unveiled

Rose Collis

CASSELL

Cassell
Villiers House, 41/47 Strand
London WC2N 5JE

387 Park Avenue South
New York, NY 10016–8810

First published 1994

British Library Cataloguing-in-Publication Data
A catalogue record for this book is available from the British Library.

Library of Congress CIP Data available

ISBN: 0–304–32853–7 (hardback)
　　　0–304–32851–0 (paperback)

Typeset by Fakenham Photosetting Ltd, Fakenham, Norfolk
Printed and bound in Great Britain by Mackays of Chatham PLC

Contents

About the Author

Rose Collis has not always been lucky: born in Wimbledon in 1959, she had the misfortune to be 'educated' at what was, officially, the worst secondary school in Greater London. Thus began an unconventional education leading, at first, to occasional jobs as a temporary secretary, guitar teacher, barmaid and, from 1979 to 1986, as an untrained performer, musician and writer in the theatre, performing throughout Britain and Europe.

Almost by accident, Rose then became an equally untrained, but more successful, journalist. Her interviews, features and reviews on a wide variety of subjects have been published in *City Limits*, *Time Out*, *The Independent*, *Gay Times*, *Everywoman*, *The Bookseller* and *Spare Rib*, amongst others. She was a member of the team that produced the award-winning TV documentary, *Framed Youth*, about young lesbians and gay men, and was the first lesbian co-editor of *City Limits*'s influential 'Out in the City' section, working with the late Brian Kennedy.

She has just acquired her first status symbol – a personal fax machine – and looks forward to many more. *Portraits to the Wall* is her first book. Her second, the eagerly awaited biography of Nancy Spain, will be published by Cassell in 1995.

For Thea, with love

And in fondest memory of
Don Melia
Brian Kennedy
Michael Griffiths
Julian Wastall
consigned to history before their time

Preface

THE question most frequently asked of authors about their books is 'Why?' In my case, it has been 'Who?' Or, more accurately, '*Who?*'

In 1993, at the height of the controversy caused by a *Vanity Fair* cover featuring supermodel Cindy Crawford and k. d. lang, I was rung up by a journalist from the *Sunday Telegraph*. She was writing a piece on lesbian chic and the myth that, suddenly, lesbians had become more acceptable (if only …). She had read, with surprise, that I was writing a book about famous lesbians: apart from Vita Sackville-West, Gertrude Stein and Sappho, she was unable to think of any others, with the exception of contemporary figures such as lang and Jeanette Winterson. I reeled off my list of subjects – and each one was greeted with that question: '*Who?*'

I suppose I really should not have been surprised at the level of ignorance about my chosen subjects, given the scarcity of publicly available information on many of the women I had decided to profile. It was Thomas Carlyle who said, 'The history of the world is but the biography of great men'; if my experiences in researching this book are anything to go by, his words have been taken a little too literally by many biographers and historians – the so-called 'keepers of the flame', as writer Ian Hamilton describes them.

The revered *Dictionary of National Biography* (Oxford University Press, 1993) only managed to increase the percentage of entries on women to 12 per cent in its *Missing Persons* volume. It never ceased to amaze me that, in many encyclopaedias or directories of art, Rosa Bonheur was not even listed. At the time of writing, only one recording of any of Ethel Smyth's work is available, a sort of Smyth-sampler CD on which the sole complete work is the *March of the Women*. Apart from Eve Balfour's *The Living*

Soil and a couple of history textbooks featuring Queen Anne, every book written by or about the women included herein is out of print and usually available only from the restricted shelves of the British Library. Although much of Selma Lagerlöf's fiction was translated into English, none of her books was available through my own local library (where incidentally, I bought my copy of Maureen Colquhoun's autobiography for 50p in an 'ex-library stock' sale). And it's not always the fault of male historians, either. In one book, *Women's History of the World* by Rosalind Miles (Michael Joseph, 1988), there were 476 entries, only four of whom were women known to be lesbians: Rosa Bonheur, Sappho, Ethel Smyth and the American film director Dorothy Arzner. Four entries, out of nearly five hundred. Even in Dale Spender's admirable *Women of Ideas and What Men Have Done to Them*, only Frances Power Cobbe and Radclyffe Hall get more than a passing mention. It is a depressing fact that, as women have been omitted from many male accounts of history, so have lesbians been sifted out of many female versions.

Apart from addressing the questions of 'who' and 'why', any book on lesbians in history has to tackle the dual problems of definition and visibility: 'How do you know?' and 'How can you find out?'

In the introduction to *Not a Passing Phase* by the Lesbian History Group, the problem of definition is referred to as 'the standard of proof', an acknowledgement that a higher level of evidence is always required of biographers and historians because of society's reluctance to recognize or admit lesbians. And, of course, the 'proof' required is unequivocal evidence of sex between the women involved – virtually impossible in most cases. Indeed, from my research, the only woman mentioned in this book (and then not as the subject of a chapter) who wrote explicitly about having sex with other women was, almost inevitably, Vita Sackville-West. Of course, this is in keeping with a broad literary tradition in which male biographers and autobiographers have written about their sexual lives in greater detail than women, even heterosexual women. But, in recent years, lesbian historians are eschewing both the definition of 'lesbian' as, in the words of the Lesbian History Group, 'only applying to women who had genital connection with each other', and the pressure to provide more 'proof' than would be demanded of heterosexual subjects. Take the example of Eve Balfour: I gathered conflicting testimony about whether she fulfilled the clinical, textbook definition of 'genital connection'. What we know for certain is that she lived all of her adult life in all-women households, all her major work partnerships were with women and, as *Country Living* put it, she 'was never seriously interested in marriage or children and is content now to live alone since the death of her close [female] friend of 50 years'. As Frankie Howerd would say, 'Please yourselves.'

The list of those to be included in this book underwent several extensive revisions. Indeed, the final decisions about one or two inclusions were not made until a matter of weeks before the publisher's deadline. My primary consideration was to assemble a reasonably balanced mixture of women from this country and mainland Europe, of the famous and the lesser known, and also of diverse achievements and talents. I hope that, given limited time, resources and space, I have achieved that balance. I must also add that, since I am not an academic, I did not stray off my reservation: that of combining as much research as possible with an accessible style of writing, in the hope of producing an informative and entertaining read. Several years ago, someone described my style of journalism as drawing on 'street vernacular' – quite the nicest way anyone's ever found of saying, 'You're from the gutter – and it *shows*.' A famous quotation including the words 'gutter' and 'stars' springs to mind ...

Right from the outset, I wanted the focus of this book to switch away from American lesbians in history to those on this side of the pond. If that sounds slightly xenophobic, it was certainly not what lay behind the concept of this book. The simple fact is that the majority of books on lesbian history have tended to be written by and about American women, which is all well and good, but lesbian booksellers in Britain have confirmed that there has been a yawning gap on their shelves for many years. Although this book is in no way intended to be a definitive work (how can any lesbian history book be so?), I hope it can play its part in filling that gap.

Whenever I solicited opinions about the book's concept and format, people would say, 'Oh, who are you doing? Radclyffe Hall?

Gertrude Stein? Natalie Barney? ...' The last two, of course, fell outside the geographical parameters of this book and, as for the first, I soon realized I'd rather have my teeth pulled than add another word to the copious volumes already written about her. Yes, she was important, yes, she was influential, but I felt I had little new to say or to reveal about possibly the most famous lesbian in history. The same applied to figures such as Anne Lister and Sappho. Inevitably, I expect to be asked, 'Why didn't you include ____?' (insert your own favourite). Suffice it to say that there would certainly be enough candidates for *Portraits to the Wall II – The Revenge*. One notable omission from this book is Nancy Spain, but for a very good reason. After nearly seven years of on-off research, I am currently writing her biography (to be published by Cassell in 1995) to coincide with the fortieth anniversary of *She*, the magazine founded by Spain and her partner, Joan Werner Laurie.

As *Portraits* progressed, I noticed a pattern of links emerging between many of the women I was writing about. Written down, it spookily resembled a game of lesbian consequences, which went:

> Frances Power Cobbe went to Italy where she met:
>
> Rosa Bonheur, who was impersonated by:
>
> Edy Craig, who was involved in the suffragette movement alongside:
>
> Ethel Smyth, who wrote about Eve Balfour's struggle against 'Queen Anne's Bounty' (the tithe) and requested librettos from:
>
> Selma Lagerlöf, who wrote a novel adapted for the screen which starred:
>
> Greta Garbo, lover of:
>
> Mercedes De Acosta ...

Admittedly, the chain breaks down a little with Catherina Linck and Maureen Colquhoun, except that Linck, like Rosa Bonheur, was arrested for wearing male attire. As for Colquhoun, her experiences with her Labour Party 'comrades' and the media seemed to encapsulate all the women's myriad problems and achievements. I would have liked to elaborate on this point, among others, with Colquhoun herself but, unfortunately, despite repeated attempts at contact, I was unable to obtain an interview with her. I would gladly welcome an opportunity to remedy this in any future edition of the book.

As I have said before, this book could never be the definitive work on lesbian lives. But I hope it will be one in a series that continues the tradition pioneered by two of my favourite books, Jane Rule's *Lesbian Images* and *The Pink Plaque Guide to London*, by Michael Elliman and Frederick Roll. I do not believe there can ever be enough books about lesbian and gay history. By the time all the hidden histories and personalities in every country have been researched, revealed and revelled in, the cycle will simply begin again. Those of us alive now are part of a history that in thirty, fifty or even a hundred years' time will, hopefully, be chronicled by others attempting to ensure that our lives, loves, achievements and struggles are not forgotten or buried in a similar fashion to those who preceded us – including the inspirational women in this book.

In the film *The Ploughman's Lunch*, one of the characters, Ann Barrington, declares, 'We must all be historians'. This was said in the context of socialist history but it is equally true in the context of lesbian history – that layer of women's history so often left buried until it becomes almost indistinguishable. The American writer, Joan Nestle, founder of New York's Lesbian Herstory Archives, summed it up beautifully when she said, 'As a woman, as a Lesbian, as a Jew, I know that much of what I call history others will not. But answering that challenge of exclusion is the work of a lifetime.' I can find no better answer to those questions, 'Why?' and 'Who?'

Rose Collis
London, January 1994

Acknowledgements

M Y thanks, in the first place, go to Linda Gibson, founding editor of *Shebang*, who originally commissioned me to write the 'Herstory' columns from which I developed the idea for this book. So now you know who to blame...

I would like to thank all at Cassell: my commissioning editor, Steve Cook, consultant editors Liz Gibbs and Peter Tatchell and, in particular, Roz Hopkins, for their encouragement and advice. I am also indebted to those who gave me vital pointers, tips and information: Peter Burton, Tom Sargant, Brighton Ourstory Project, Mark Bunyan, Lady Kathleen Oldfield and, especially, Ann Cahill of the Soil Association and Mary Langman of the Wholefood Trust. As well as those already mentioned, my thanks, as always, go to Helen Dady, Chris Moller, Sue Brearley, Tom Robinson, Mandy McCartin, Lucy McPhail and Ian Shaw for their treasured friendship and encouragement. Finally, my thanks go to Thea Bennett, for a vital copy of *Country Living* and for her love and support.

You don't change the course of history by turning the faces of portraits to the wall.

Jawaharlal Nehru

History is a gallery of pictures in which there are few originals and many copies.

Alexis de Tocqueville

Catherina Linck and Catherina Muhlhahn

LOOK in any book of quotations under the heading 'history' and there are always dozens of entries, ranging from the profound to the petulant. But there are two quotes which rarely appear in such sections but which should. First, 'those who do not remember history are condemned to repeat it'. Secondly, as mafioso Michael Corleone (played by Al Pacino) told an aide in *Godfather II*, 'Nothing is impossible. If history has taught us anything, it's that you can kill anyone.' For any strands of any society in any country who have been persecuted for simply existing (especially lesbians and gay men), these must be the two most vital history lessons to learn. And so they should: because history has a nasty habit of returning to teach us unlearned lessons – usually the hard way. For instance, it is easy to discount the possibility that the shadows of judicial murders carried out in the Middle Ages could stretch across the centuries almost into the third millennium – but then, as we should know, nothing is impossible and if history does not condemn us to repetition, it can repeat its condemnations.

In September 1991, at Doncaster Crown Court, eighteen-year-old Jennifer Saunders was sentenced to six years' imprisonment on two charges of indecently assaulting two other women. The presiding judge, Justice Jonathan Crabtree, said at the trial, 'I suspect these girls would rather have been raped by some young man than have happen to them what you did.' Of course, six years' jail was much longer than most convicted rapists receive. The judge's comments caused an outcry and, though he backed down, he stood by the severe sentence, saying it would act as a deterrent:

'In these days of openness about lesbianism and bisexual behaviour it will ensure that anybody else who is tempted to try and copy what you do will count the cost.'

Saunders was sixteen at the time of her affairs and always denied the allegations, maintaining that both women knew she was a lesbian and that she had agreed to dress as a boy and call herself 'Jimmy' to hide their sexuality from one set of parents. One of her former girlfriends said in court that, during their five-month relationship, she and 'Jimmy' had sex more than twenty times and that she believed 'he' had a cancer on one side of his chest, a boil on the other and that his 'penis' could not be touched by her because of an 'operation'. In June 1992, a High Court judge heard Saunders' appeal and reduced her sentence to two years' probation. Saunders' counsel had advised her to appeal only against the sentence, rather than the convictions themselves.

Her sentence was horrendous and her case, rightly, became the focus of an international lesbian campaign, with support coming from Holland and Germany. However, severe penalties for lesbians in similar cases had widespread – and often fatal – precedents in mainland Europe as recently as two centuries ago.

There was no uniform teaching against homosexuality in Christianity's first millennium. The turning-point appears to have been in the thirteenth century when European society outlawed any sort of religious – and, therefore, social – nonconformity. It was the time of the Spanish Inquisition and the first persecution of European Jews. During this century, virtually every law which penalized gays had a twin law which penalized Jews, thus predating the persecution suffered by these two sections of society under Hitler with eerie and depressing accuracy.

Most laws criminalizing homosexuality were created between 1150 and 1250 but they remained on the statute books of many European countries until the eighteenth and nineteenth centuries, and in some notorious cases (stand up, Britain), even into this century. And here comes the question: do religion and law bend to the will of the people or vice versa? Why attitudes changed so drastically in the thirteenth century had more to do with Christianity's attitude towards love, rather than sex. Love had no place within marriage, and marital sex was for procreation. Outside marriage was the place for romantic, if non-carnal, love. During the twelfth century, a wealth of poetry, expressing this love, was produced, most of it emanating from monastery and convent communities. Eventually, the ecclesiastical hierarchy must have realized that these unmarried people were having too much of a good time and, towards the end of the century, the conventional wisdom became that love within marriage was acceptable and, moreover, that marriage was the *only* place for love.

So where did all the trouble start? The answer is surprisingly simple – with St Paul. In Romans 1:26, condemning transgressors and their myriad sins, he sneered, 'for even their women did change the natural use into that which is against nature'.[1] In other translations this is given as 'their women exchanged natural relations for unnatural'. In 1 Corinthians 6:9–11, Paul decreed that 'neither the immoral, nor idolaters, nor adulterers, nor homosexuals ... will inherit the kingdom of God'.[2] The tenor of Paul's views on homosexuality was that gay sex was not merely sinful but a sign of false religion, and that it went against the basic teachings of Leviticus, which warned that 'ye shall have no other gods but me'.

Down the years, theologians have offered up some very free interpretations of Romans and these in turn have been used as the basis of institutionalized religion's unholy war against homosexuals – a justification for Christendom's judicial murder of those it regarded as sexual heretics. Even in the late twentieth century, we have seen how bibles and other religious tracts are readily produced and thumped by frighteningly fanatical queer-fearers, whose devotion to questionable deities and equally spurious texts outweighs any regard for the toleration of other human beings and their entitlement to rights and justice.

The fourth-century theologian St John Chrysostom was in no doubt that Paul's writings were directed against lesbians and took them to mean that tribadism was even more disgraceful than sodomy because women ought to have more shame than men.

In AD 423 St Augustine wrote to a group of nuns, warning of the dangers of their all-woman, close-knit community: 'The love which you bear one another ought not to be carnal, but spiritual; for those things which are practised by immodest women, even with other females, ought not to be done even by married women or by girls who are about to marry ...'[3]

An Italian theologian, Peter Damiani, published the *Liber Gomorrhianus* in 1051, which condemned male homosexuality but not lesbianism. However, St Anselm of Canterbury in the twelfth century supported St Paul's condemnation of lesbians 'because the women themselves committed shameful deeds with women'.[4]

In the next century, St Thomas Aquinas, one of the biggest influences on Catholic moral ethics, listed four types of 'unnatural vice' in his *Summa Theologiae*, including 'female with female, as the Apostle states (Rom. 1:27): and this is called the vice of sodomy'.[5] However, even Aquinas regarded homosexuality as a natural phenomenon, a defect or quirk of nature.

Another important theological code of conduct was the 'Penitentials', which originated in Ireland and Wales around the seventh century and are significant because they appear to be the first laws which specifically recognized – and penalized – lesbians. The Penitentials influenced the laws of punishment in England, France, Germany and Italy for nearly five hundred years. According to this code, the sins for which penalties could be applied were 'one lay woman indulging in homosexual acts with another' and 'nuns using an artificial phallus'.[6] The latter is so specific it almost smacks of collusion! But the punishments for being caught in the act were hardly frivolous: lay women received a penance of three years, while their holier sisters received seven years. In Renaissance Italy, an abbess, Sister Benedetta Carlini, was convicted of forcing younger nuns to have sex with her by impersonating a male angel, 'Splenditello'. For the last forty years of her life she was in solitary confinement within the abbey, fed sporadically on bread and water and allowed out only to attend Mass or to be flogged.

Other penitentials singled out lesbianism as a sin, including writings by Theodore of Tarsus, Archbishop of Canterbury in the seventh century. The infamous preacher John Calvin wrote several appraisals of the writings of St Paul. In his 'Commentary on First Corinthians 6:9–11', he described the sexual sin mentioned in verse 9 as 'the most serious of all, viz, that unnatural and filthy thing which was far too common in Greece'.[7] Clearly, he didn't mean sunbathing.

7: *Catherina Linck and Catherina Muhlhahn*

In medieval Italy, the essence of Roman Imperial law began to be revived by jurists. One of these was Cino da Pistoia, who interpreted one law, the *lex foedissima*, as pertaining to lesbians: 'The laws punish the most foul wickedness of women who surrender their honour to the lusts of others'.[8] Although this edict is ambiguous, to say the least, Cino was adamant that it not only meant women who had sex with men: 'For there are certain women, inclined to foul wickedness, who exercise their lust on other women and pursue them like men.'[9] Yet another jurist, Bartholomaeus de Saliceto, not only agreed with Cino's conclusions but recommended that the death penalty should be applied to such women, citing another Roman law that punished male homosexuals with the 'avenging sword'.[10]

The influence of Roman law was not confined to Italy: crimes and punishments based on it were found in France, Spain, Germany and Scotland up to the seventeenth century. Medieval Spain seemed particularly keen on punishing lesbians for sodomy as well as men under its Las Siete Partidas. Early editions, prepared by one Gregorio Lopez in 1555, condemned lesbians to the same penalty – death – as men, citing St Paul as justification. Another, Antonio Gomez, also advocated punishment for women who acted 'the part of the man with another woman', again claiming Saints Paul and Thomas Aquinas as the precedents. However, he suggested that there be two tiers of penalties: if a woman had sex with another 'by means of any material instrument', they both were to be burned at the stake. If no such 'instrument' was used, the punishment would be lighter – this probably meant being flogged and sent to the galleys.[11]

The ease and frequency with which the scripture-based laws of some European countries were picked up by others is a sobering reminder of why, in the last ten years, alarm spread through the lesbian and gay communities of Germany and Holland when the British government began to step up its legislative war against homosexuality with, for instance, Section 28 of the Local Government Act. The rallies, the fund-raising events and the letters of protest that came from mainland Europe when these spectres were raised showed that not everyone was prepared to forget how quickly malevolent influences spread and how the whole of Christendom founded its justification for judicial murder.

The fact that lesbians were not persecuted with such obvious zeal as male homosexuals reflects the prevailing view of society that women were far from equal to men. After all, it was that infamous Catholic heretic, Luther, who stated that 'A woman is never truly her own master. God formed her body to belong to a man, to have and to rear children. Let them bear children till they die of it. That is what they are for.'[12] Prior to the French Revolution, in France, Spain, Italy, Germany and Switzerland, lesbian sex was regarded as legally equal to male sodomy, for which the punishment was death. Under the reign of Louis IX in the thirteenth century, a national penal code, Les Etablissements de Saint Louis, was formed out of the common laws of a number of regions, including Orléans, Anjou and Maine. One part of the code was aimed against heretics, and under this statute the following punishments were decreed for lesbians: 'A woman who does this shall undergo mutilation for the first and second offences/lose her member each time, and on the third must be burned. And all the goods of such offenders shall be the king's.'[13] Quite what is intended by 'member' is unclear: it may have meant the loss of an arm or leg. The few documented cases show that the severest penalty was indeed applied:

- In 1477, in Speier, Germany, a young woman was drowned 'for lesbian love'.
- In Italy in 1580, a woman was hanged for dressing as a man and 'marrying' a woman.
- In France, a woman was burned at the stake in 1535 for the same 'offence'.
- In 1533, two women were tortured and put on trial in Bordeaux, but were eventually acquitted because of insufficient evidence.
- In Fontaine in 1535, a woman was burned at the stake after she was discovered to have married another woman.
- In Marne, Italy, in 1580, another woman was hanged for the same reason.

It was in Germany, several centuries later, that a trial occurred that was the predecessor of Jennifer Saunders' treatment.

In 1721, in the Saxony town of Halberstadt, Catherina Margaretha Linck and Catherina Margaretha Muhlhahn were put on trial for sodomy. A detailed account of not only their trial but also Linck's life was published in 1891 by a Dr F. C. Müller, taken from the Prussian Secret Archives, which contained records of over a hundred sodomy trials. A translation of Müller's paper was produced by lesbian historian, Brigitte Eriksson, in 1981.[14]

Linck was born in 1694 in Gehowen, out of wedlock, and sent to an orphanage in Halle. At fourteen, she went to work as a button-maker in Calbe, but soon decided to embark on a holy life instead. Dressing in male attire, she joined a religious sect, the Inspirants, who were much given to ecstatic gatherings, self-inflicted penances and prophesying. Linck showed signs of being a prodigious prophet but her gifts quickly waned. Within months, she joined the Hanoverian troops as a musketeer, under the name Anastasius Lagranas Caspar Beuerlein. In 1708, after three years, she deserted, was captured near Antwerp and condemned to die at the gallows. But the revelation of her true sex saved her – a great irony, given later events.

Before long she enlisted again, this time with the Volunteer Company of the Royal Prussian troops in Soest but, after a year, she was again identified as a woman and discharged. For the next twelve months she made a half-hearted effort to conform, returning to Halle and wearing female attire. It did not last and she joined the Royal Polish troops as a musketeer under the name of Peter Wannich. During a battle she was captured by French troops but managed to escape and this time joined the Hessian troops. Once more, she absconded and returned, in male guise, to Halle, where she worked for the university shoemaker and as a supervisor in the cotton spinning and printing trade. In 1717, she went to work for a French stocking-maker in Halberstadt, where she met Catherina Muhlhahn. They quickly became engaged and were married later that year.

According to the translated trial documents, Linck had constructed an ingenious set of false wedding tackle, consisting of a stuffed leather cock and a pig's bladder scrotum, attached with a leather strap. Thus equipped, she is said (according to the prosecution) to have announced to her bride on her wedding night that 'she wanted to have intercourse 24 times but she had done so only three or four times'.[15]

It appears that their relationship deteriorated rather rapidly, due in some part to lack of money, but also undoubtedly to living with the knowledge of what their fates would be if they were found out. Given that Linck had been more or less steadily employed since she was fourteen, it can only be surmised that she could not take another job for fear of her true sex – and consequently the real nature of her relationship with Muhlhahn – being discovered again. The two women criss-crossed the country, living cheaply, their only income derived from begging. After returning to Halberstadt, they eventually decided that their financial prospects would improve if Linck was a recognized Catholic, rather than a former Inspirant, and so she set off, alone, to the city of Helmstadt for instruction and baptism.

Meanwhile, a weary and ailing Muhlhahn had returned to live with her mother, who once before had tried to force the couple to divorce, for reasons which remain unclear. Perhaps her mother's intuition had led her to guess the true nature of their relationship and, as well as her own feelings of revulsion, she was keenly aware of the punishment her daughter might face as a result. Obtaining a divorce would, at least, save her from the gallows and, regardless of how she felt about Catherina being a lesbian, this would surely have been Mrs Muhlhahn's primary concern.

However, what she had not bargained for was the depth of love between the two Catherinas. Despite their tempestuous relationship and separations, there was obviously a deep bond between them and a 'divorce' was out of the question. It appears that at some point, when Mrs Muhlhahn finally grasped this fact, her patience ran out. It may even be that, when her daughter returned to the family bosom, distraught after another row with Linck, she gave away their big secret. Whatever the precipitation, it led to a violent and ultimately tragic confrontation when the newly baptized Linck next came to visit her 'wife'. Muhlhahn's mother accused her of not being a man, and in the ensuing furore, she and another woman attacked Linck, ripped her trousers open and tore off her leather appendage. This was submitted to the authorities, along with a beaten and bruised Linck. Mrs Muhlhahn's attempts to protect her daughter failed disastrously when she, too, was put on trial for sodomy. Both women quickly confessed their 'sins', perhaps in the vain hope that a *mea culpa* attitude would persuade the authorities to be lenient.

During her subsequent interrogation, Linck maintained that Muhlhahn and her mother had always known she was a woman. She claimed that Muhlhahn had removed the leather phallus from her body before but continued to have sex with her and, when the two lovers were confronted with each other, Linck claimed her 'wife' had seen her fully naked. However, Muhlhahn protested that she thought her 'husband' had been a man all along, and that when she fondled Linck's bosom, it was in the belief that 'many men had such breasts'. In desperation, Linck claimed that her sins were the result of having been 'deluded by Satan'.

It was all to no avail: despite a plea from the defending counsel for life imprisonment for Linck and acquittal for Muhlhahn, the Duisberg Judicial Faculty ordered, respectively, execution and 'serious punishment'. The Halberstadt municipal government condoned the sentences, citing Linck's offences as 'hideous and nasty' and certainly enough to warrant capital punishment. She was to be hanged and her body burned. To add insult to mortal injury, she was also ordered to pay two-thirds of the court costs incurred. Her lover and co-defendant was condemned to 'second-degree torture in order to arrive at the truth in her case'. On appeal, this was reduced to 'three years in the penitentiary or spinning room and afterwards [she] should be banished from the country'.[16]

There is no record of what became of Catherina Muhlhahn after her imprisonment and banishment. However, there is no doubt that life would have become even grimmer: convicted and punished for what was then considered a heinous crime, physically weakened and spiritually humiliated by incarceration and refused leave to stay in her own country, it is unlikely she made old bones. Even if she survived prison, what prospects could there have been for her, an unmarried foreign woman, branded for life and with no means or skills, friendless and cut off from her family? As if this was not enough, we can only guess at how she must have felt after having to denounce and sacrifice the woman she once loved in a desperate attempt to save her own neck. Although her selfish actions may appear to be wantonly cruel and callous, who can now put their hand on their heart and say that, in those circumstances, they would have acted any differently? After all, nearly three hundred years after Catherina Linck was sacrificed to religious beliefs, Jennifer Saunders' teenage lovers were quick enough to throw her to the legal lions to save themselves from their families' wrath. If someone can put the fear of God into you, you are capable of killing anyone.

Notes

1. *The Bible*, Revised Standard Version (London, 1952).
2. *Ibid.*
3. Derrick Bailey, *Homosexuality and the Western Christian Tradition* (London, Longmans, 1955), p. 161.
4. Salvatore J. Licata and Robert P. Paterson (eds), *The Gay Past* (New York, Harrington Park Press, 1981), p. 36.
5. *Ibid.*
6. Bailey, *Homosexuality*.
7. Richard F. Lovelace, *Homosexuality and the Church* (London, Lamp Press, 1979), p. 47.
8. Licata and Paterson, *Gay Past*, p. 30.
9. *Ibid.*
10. *Ibid.*
11. *Ibid.*
12. Martin Luther, *Kritische Gesamtausgabe*, Vol. 3, Briefwechsel (Weimar, Hermann Bohlaus Nachf, 1933).
13. Bailey, *Homosexuality*, p. 161.
14. Brigitte Eriksson, in Licata and Paterson, *Gay Past*, pp. 27 ff.
15. *Ibid.*
16. *Ibid.*

Queen Anne and
Sarah Churchill

THE House of Windsor has provided its fair share of news fodder in the 1990s. From 'Camillagate' to 'Squidgygate', Royal scandals have become commonplace. There have, of course, been similar events before (the circumstances surrounding the abdication of Edward VIII spring to mind), but there has been one crucial factor in the latest batch that the others lacked: the existence of the voracious tabloid print and electronic media, feeding an emotionally, spiritually and intellectually parched mass audience. Before the onset of modern media, mass communication might have meant commemorating the news of the day in popular ballads and verse, sung in taverns, wash-houses and backyards. Nowadays, ballads have been swapped for button-controls, which, with a minimum of prompting, summon up computer games, videos and television programming that aims for (and hits) the lowest common denominator, arm-in-arm with a yellow press that seeks to educate and inform with headlines and pictures only.

It's a pity for them they didn't exist 250 years ago; they would have had even more of a field day than they did with 'Topless Fergie's Foot-Kisser' and 'Saint Diana's Dead Marriage'. What fun they could have had following the antics of the last Stuart monarch, Queen Anne, as she ruffled the stately feathers of Court and country by her open and passionate preference for Sarah Churchill, née Jennings, first Duchess of Marlborough.

Anne was born in St James's Palace, London, in 1665, the year of the plague. Her parents, James, Duke of York (later James II) and Anne Hyde, had eight children but only Anne and her sister,

Mary, survived. After his wife's death, James converted to Catholicism and his daughters were sent to Richmond Palace by Charles II to be raised in the Church of England under the tuition of the Bishop of London. Despite avoiding the plague and the early demise of her brothers and sisters, Anne's health was always weak. When she was four, she suffered from a serious eye infection which left her short-sighted and with a permanent frown. The infection recurred throughout her life and left her able to read very little.

The image of Anne's childhood is sad: her mother died at an early age and she detested her stepmother, Mary of Modena. Scant attention was paid to her or her education, which consisted mainly of sewing and embroidery, music and religion, but not even the most basic grammar. The Crown eventually passed to her sister, Queen Mary II, and King William, but they produced no heirs and so Anne became heir to the throne. Even so, her schooling included nothing of politics, history or anything else that befitted a future monarch. This sickly, orphaned and lonely girl lived in fear of whispered Catholic conspiracies (most notably, the plot to make the Duke of Monmouth heir to the throne), and most of her friendships were fairly transient. Except one.

When she was five, she was introduced to a lively ten-year-old girl who was one of her stepmother's maids-of-honour. Anne was immediately smitten: Sarah Jennings later recalled, 'She even then expressed a particular fondness for me. This inclination increased with our years.'[1] Sarah's more famous descendant, Sir Winston Churchill, wrote of the 'romantic, indeed perfervid element in Anne's love for Sarah, to which the elder girl responded warmly several years before she realised the worldly importance of such a relationship'. Historians have remained divided on the subject: some have described Anne's feelings for Sarah as 'weird, obsessive, erotic', while others have reflected, 'These things happen. And what more natural?' Anne wanted no standing on ceremony and insisted on equality and informality in their relations. Sarah later wrote, 'She grew uneasy to be treated by me with the form and ceremony due to her rank.' In letters, Anne insisted on ordinary nicknames: Sarah became 'Mrs Freeman', Anne was 'Mrs Morley'.

The Bishop of Salisbury wrote of Sarah that she had become 'so great a favourite with the Princess that she seemed to be the mistress of her whole heart and thoughts'.[2] For her part, Anne wrote to her 'dear Mrs Freeman', 'I swear I would live on bread and water between four walls with her without repining.' Other letters contained equally impassioned declarations: 'Nothing but death can ever make me part with you. For if it be possible, I am every day more and more yours.'[3] Yet another promised, 'Be assured if you should ever do so cruel a thing as to leave me ... I will shut myself up and never see the world more.'[4]

Despite such passionate pleas of commitment, Sarah married the man who was to become one of Anne's most successful military campaigners, John Churchill, an ambitious warrior who never lost a single battle. Initially, Sarah was unimpressed by him, but they were eventually married in secret when she was eighteen. Marlborough had fallen out of favour with Mary and William after he had helped quell a rebellion on the Irish mainland. Although he was made an earl, he considered that he had not been properly rewarded for his efforts and began to associate with those who were critical of the King. It seems that William was not particularly troubled by this behaviour, although Marlborough was incarcerated in the Tower of London for a brief spell, but Mary was furious and made several attempts to persuade Anne that Sarah should not be at Court, even threatening to reduce her sister's allowance. Anne resisted and left Court, taking Sarah with her. After Mary's death, she and the Churchills were reconciled with the King.

Anne was married in 1683 to the rather dull Prince George of Denmark, a pleasant enough soul but the laughing stock of the Court, known as '*Est-il possible?*' to all and sundry because that was generally all he had to contribute to conversations. For a joke, he was elected High Steward of Colchester, a job which Sarah considered 'a mighty proper employment for the Queen's husband'.[5] Her Majesty, though, was not amused. Anne had a decent enough relationship with her husband, but her involvement with Sarah Churchill remained intense and dominant.

So, with her strong, confident personality, her wit and her beauty, Sarah netted not only a prize husband but the passionate love and devotion of the heir to the throne. In doing so, she became the most prestigious and powerful woman in the country, second only to Anne herself.

Anne's already frail health was ruined by a horrendous series of annual pregnancies – seventeen in total, and all but one resulting in miscarriage or stillbirth. The only surviving child, William, Duke of Gloucester, died when he was eleven. When the coffin of Mary, Queen of Scots, was discovered in a crowded catacomb in Westminster Abbey in the nineteenth century, it was surrounded by dozens of tiny children's coffins, including the off-spring of Anne. The appalling succession of doomed pregnancies, the early death of young Gloucester and Anne's so-called 'gout' may well have been due to hereditary syphilis, passed on from either her father or husband. Whatever the reason, by the time she was thirty, Anne was a virtual invalid. As chief mourner, she should have followed the cortège at Queen Mary's funeral but she was unable to walk. And at her own coronation, in 1702, she had to be carried for most of the procession.

Given the rather miserable existence her ailments con-demned her to, she can hardly be blamed for finding so much pleasure in food. She was known to eat an entire fowl for dinner, as well as dishes before and after. Even before she came to the throne, a popular rhyme declared:

> *King William thinks all*
> *Queen Mary talks all*
> *Prince George drinks all*
> *And Princess Anne eats all*

Though she was not known for drinking heavily, it was rumoured that she was fond of sipping brandy out of a teacup, and jokes were made about 'Queen Anne's cold tea'.

While his wife remained in favour with Anne, John Churchill also prospered, as did his friends. One of the closest, Sidney Godolphin, was made Anne's first Lord Treasurer (equival-ent to Prime Minister) and, within days of her coronation, England was at war with France and Spain, providing Churchill with the opportunity to make his mark as the Queen's finest soldier. Anne subsequently made him first Duke of Marlborough and showered the family with substantial gifts and bequests, estimated at one time to total £65,000 a year.

After Marlborough's famous victory at Blenheim in 1704, she gave them the 15,000-acre royal estate at Woodstock, in Oxfordshire. On this would be built (at government expense) Blenheim Palace, home of subsequent generations of Churchills. A statue of Anne still stands there as a fitting reminder of how and why the family's stately home came courtesy of a stately homo. Anne also provided the site for Sarah's London home, Marlborough House, which was conveniently located next door to St James's Palace. Sir Christopher Wren was originally hired to design the house but Sarah sacked him and took on the job herself. The bricks for Marlborough House were brought from Holland, where the Duke scored many of his famous military victories. Similarly, she dismissed the architect of Blenheim Palace, Sir John Vanbrugh, and took over the supervision of its construction.

Anne's love for, and dependency on, Sarah was an open secret in Court and out: one popular broadsheet of the time declared, 'And Anne shall wear the Crown, but Sarah reign'. Anne was still telling Sarah, 'Nothing can ever express how passionately I am yours.'[6] But the matter had become a good deal more complex than it had been when the women were young girls in the first flush of love. While Anne's marriage and subsequent pregnancies did not make a dent in her feelings for Sarah, Sarah's emotional energy was increasingly poured into securing the future of her own children and grandchildren. Some historians have intimated that Sarah did not fully reciprocate Anne's feelings, who was wont, particularly in the first years of their relationship, to write overly sentimental and gushing letters. However, when the two women fell out, Sarah had no compunction in making Anne reread these letters in a clumsy attempt to heal the rift. We do not know if Sarah's correspondence was as impassioned; she stipulated that all her letters to Anne were to be destroyed once they had been read. It was only after they had fallen out that Sarah kept copies of her letters to the Queen. We can never really know the true depth of Sarah's feelings for Anne; what we can observe, though, is Anne's side of the relationship, which spoke of a deep involvement that was ruined once she came to the throne. She longed for them to be young women again and to live as they had done when their relationship was at its most intimate, before the complex, troubled affairs of state and Sarah's dynastic ambitions swept the romance away.

Nonetheless, when Anne first appeared as Queen in the House of Lords, Marlborough carried the Sword of State ahead of her, followed by Sarah. When Anne became Queen, Sarah was appointed Lady of the Bedchamber, Mistress of the Robes, Groom of the Stole and Keeper of the Privy Purse and, on the outbreak of war with France, Marlborough was given command of the English and Dutch armies.

Meanwhile, poor Anne's body continued to deteriorate. She needed a specially designed chair to lift her into her coach and, at Windsor Castle, an elaborate pulley mechanism took her from floor to floor. She loved stag hunting but could often only follow the hunt carried along in a strange, wheeled contraption. However, she regularly attended the House of Lords and the weekly meetings of the Cabinet Council. She was also concerned about her people, and routinely read petitions from convicts who had been sentenced to death or exile, often pleading clemency for them with the appropriate minister. When she was not busy trying to spend time with Sarah or struggling to deal with the complex affairs of state, Anne would read religious texts and occasionally some histories of England. Sometimes, she would watch the deer in the Royal Parks or review the troops.

Her appearance and behaviour were the butt of many cruel comments. Prone to blushing, a popular joke described her as looking like the sign of the Rose and Crown. But, despite her terrible state of health and swollen appearance, Anne was portrayed in most of the portraits of the day as majestically beautiful and all-conquering. Many of the images were created in celebration of some victory or other over the French and, specifically, Louis XIV. A 1709 painting showed her riding a chariot over the French King and the Pope. On a medal commemorating the capture of Donay in 1710, Anne is portrayed as Delilah cutting off Louis' hair; on the reverse side, she plays a harp while he dances to her tune. Other images of her depicted events a little closer to home. One pack of playing cards bore several images of Anne: on the ten, she is shown dismissing one of her ladies and appointing another. The caption reads: 'Her Majesty her Self of Trouble eases/And Chuses such Attendants as She pleases'.

Inevitably, it was the flux and change of the high politics of the times – plus a little old-fashioned jealousy – that would drive a wedge between Anne and Sarah. Anne favoured the Tories because they supported the Church and Royal supremacy, while Sarah grew closer to the Whigs, who challenged the notion of the divine right of sovereign succession. For a number of years, she vainly attempted to convince Anne of the Whigs' virtues but Anne, though she laid the foundations for a multi-party Parliament, regarded the Whigs as pure Republicans. Moreover, they had been the prime instigators behind an unsuccessful attempt to remove her from the line of succession when she was a child.

Sarah was also becoming increasingly tired of Anne's possessiveness, and her absences from Court became longer and more frequent. Given this, it is hardly surprising that she soon found herself supplanted by a cousin and one of her former protégées, Abigail Hill, who merely sat, sewed, smiled and sang, and, more importantly, made no attempt to change her Queen's political persuasions. Sarah later wrote that, in 1706, Anne 'saw Mrs Hill every day in private, and never did me'.[7]

Sarah was outraged by Abigail's swift rise. It was she who, before Anne's accession, had discovered that Abigail was working as a domestic servant and secured her a position as a bedchamber-woman to the Princess. Although it was still a menial job, it carried some prestige and would usually have been unobtainable by domestics; two of Sarah's daughters also held this position. Even so, Abigail's new job involved such intimate duties as sleeping on the floor of Anne's bedroom and, in the morning, disposing of the Royal slops. Even after she became Baroness Masham, consolidating her position and influence by marrying one of Prince George's bedchamber grooms, Anne still insisted that Abigail retain her office of bedchamber-woman.

If by now Sarah found Anne physically repulsive and emotionally demanding and overbearing, why did she persist in haranguing her about Abigail Masham? What made this otherwise astute and perceptive woman act so recklessly? After getting her own way for so long, her jealousy was understandable, but if she endured Anne's affection in order to fulfil her political ambitions then she appeared to be overreacting. Perhaps, underneath all the scorn and distaste, vestiges of deep affection remained. And, of course, it may well have been a case of 'I may not want her, but that doesn't mean anyone else can have her'. Nonetheless, it is baffling that she appeared to go out of her way to court Anne's disaffection. If she had not wanted Abigail Masham to become so close to the Queen, she could easily have spent more time at Court, which would certainly have contented Anne. But Sarah simply did not have the patience; the permanently ailing Anne was too dull company for her and she obviously still felt confident enough to pursue her own ambitious agenda while remaining on good enough terms with Anne to get what she wanted from her.

Her outspokenness may well have played a major part in her downfall. According to one popular story, Abigail went to fetch a pair of Anne's gloves which she had left in a room adjoining her bedroom. Sarah was there, reading a letter, and Abigail noticed she had put on the Queen's gloves by mistake. When she pointed this out, Sarah tore them off exclaiming, 'Have I on anything that has touched the odious hands of that disagreeable woman? Take them away!'[8] Since Anne's door was wide open, she was able to hear every word of this exchange. She remained silent but, for her new favourite, it was a useful piece of ammunition in the ongoing war of attrition with her former benefactor.

Sarah was seething with jealousy: in her memoirs, she noted that, 'Mrs Masham came often to the queen when the prince was asleep, and was generally two hours every day in private with her.' She maintained that Anne did not want it made public that she spent so much time with Abigail. After Prince George died, Anne reopened two small rooms that had been used by him. Not only did they connect with a room next to Anne's dressing-room, they had a back staircase which, conveniently, led to Abigail's rooms. Using these, she could creep in and out of the Royal bedroom undetected.

Sarah bombarded Anne with letters, some taking her to task for her infatuation with Abigail. She also had no hesitation in forwarding copies of the poems and ballads, currently circulating, which concerned rumours of the Queen's relationships with women. Some of these were almost certainly written by members of the Marlborough set. They left little to the imagination:

> When as Queen Anne of great Renown
> Great Britain's Scepter sway'd
> Besides the Church, she dearly lov'd
> A Dirty Chamber-Maid
>
> Her Secretary she was not
> Because she could not write
> But had the Conduct and the Care
> Of some dark Deeds at Night

After bringing such material to Anne's attention, Sarah then proceeded to write a letter which, given the previous intimacy between them, displays remarkable hypocrisy. In it she pronounced, 'there can be no great reputation in a thing so strange and unaccountable ... having no inclination for any but of one's own sex....'[9] A phrase containing the words 'pot' and 'kettle' springs to mind. But then, of course, no written evidence existed of the exact nature of Sarah's feelings for Anne, so she must have felt safe to taunt the Queen in this way. Not long after this, a pamphlet called *The Rival Duchess* was circulated throughout London. In it, Abigail is portrayed as telling the wife of Louis XIV, 'I was rather addicted to another Sort of Passion, of having too great a Regard for my own Sex.' In her memoirs, Sarah recalled making her way to Anne's bedroom via the secret passage and finding Abigail already there. When Abigail spotted her, she immediately adopted more formal behaviour: she curtseyed, spluttered out, 'Did your Majesty ring?' and made a hasty exist.

It was all very messy, very sad and deplorably undignified, and it left the chief ministers wearily shaking their heads. Vanbrugh, with typical British understatement, told Lord Manchester, 'Things are in an odd way at Court.'

Hostilities ceased for a short while after the death of Anne's consort, Prince George, but not for long. Matters finally came to a head in August 1708 when, en route to a thanksgiving service in St Paul's for victory at the battle of Oudenarde, there was a public squabble about Anne's jewels, of all things. As Mistress of the Robes, it was Sarah who had selected and prepared the jewels which the Queen would wear for the service. In the coach Sarah noticed that Anne had not put them on and, suspecting that Abigail had had a hand in this decision, took it as a deliberate snub. Incredibly, instead of waiting until after the service, she began to berate Anne and continued her ranting on the very steps of the cathedral. When Anne tried to defend herself, Sarah told her sovereign Queen to put a Royal sock in it. She later explained that she feared the Queen would say something unfit for the ears of the waiting crowd. Not content with this affront, she then wrote to Anne about the matter and again took the opportunity to blame Abigail, claiming that it was she, Sarah, who had most reason to be offended.

It appears that everyone, except Sarah, could see it was all going to end in tears. Even her husband tried to stop her reproaching the Queen, but to no avail. Despite everything, Anne seemed to want a reconciliation and agreed to meet Sarah at Kensington Palace. She was still able to write to her former great love, 'there being nothing more desirous of than to have a thorough good understanding between dear Mrs Freeman and her poor unfortunate faithful Morley, who will till her last moment be so. . . .' Sarah went to the meeting with a long list of grievances and another list detailing her services to Queen and country. Incredibly, Sarah even made veiled threats to publish Anne's letters to her. With characteristic foresight, she had always insisted that Anne destroy the letters she had written to her, which covered the years when they had been most intimate. In the circumstances, Anne's patience was remarkable: had her love for Sarah not been so deep, another monarch might well have dispatched her to the Tower for less.

Sarah demanded to know who had turned Anne against her and what she had done wrong, to which Anne repeated, 'You desired no answer, and you shall have none.' The effect of this persistent, repetitive defence completely disarmed Sarah. Her frustration got the better of her and she told Anne that she would suffer for her 'inhumanity'. Anne replied, 'That will be to myself.'[10] These were the last words they ever said to one another.

John Churchill, aware of the implications of the situation,

urged Sarah to apologize to the Queen. Eventually, she did write a contrite letter, which Churchill himself took to Anne. But it was too little, too late: she would hardly look at the letter and told him, 'I cannot change my resolution.' Sarah was stripped of her offices: the Duchess of Somerset succeeded her as Mistress of the Robes and Groom of the Stole, and Abigail Masham was given control of the Privy Purse.

Sarah and Churchill went to live abroad, and only returned to England upon Anne's death in 1714. Anne's health was dismal for the last two years of her life but, ironically, the much-favoured Abigail may have been indirectly responsible for sending her to her deathbed. A Spanish trade treaty was due to be agreed by Parliament, but a number of Whigs queried the finer details. It was revealed that some of those closest to Anne, including Abigail, might have received substantial sums of money as reward for using their influence over the Queen to persuade her to sign the treaty. A row broke out in Parliament and, aware that her fate lay in the balance, Abigail persuaded the ailing Queen to intervene. Although she was hardly able to stand, let alone walk, Anne agreed, but the row made her worse and she was carried out. Two days later, the 'gout' reached her brain and she began to suffer convulsions. During her final illness, she was bled and her head shaved. Thankfully, she was unconscious while her physicians heaped these physical indignities on her poor, destroyed body and her ministers busied themselves with ensuring the Crown passed to the right heir. While briefly conscious, she passed her Staff of Office to the new Lord Treasurer, Lord Shrewsbury, with the instruction 'Use it for the good of my people.' They were her last words; she died on 1 August 1714, aged not quite fifty, and her pitiful swollen body was buried in Westminster Abbey in a coffin which was nearly square. Depending on which historians you choose to believe, Abigail Masham was either 'almost dead with grief' or had left the Queen's deathbed to go looting in St James's Palace.

The Churchills returned to England three days later, making a triumphant re-entry into London, cheered on by a large crowd. Sarah outlived both queen and husband and lost no time at all in ensuring that (without the benefit of her destroyed letters, of course) her version of the relationship with Anne and the subsequent falling out was written and published. She employed a professional writer, Nathaniel Hooke, to produce the final draft. It told the bitter tale of betrayal by the woman – Abigail – who (according to Sarah, at least) owed her everything. It was also this publication that perpetuated the view of Anne as a weak and stupid monarch.

Sarah refused to be drawn on how history would judge her dead friend. She commented: 'Whether her memory will be celebrated by posterity with blessings or curses, time will show.' And what *was* Anne remembered for? The Scots probably remember her (none too kindly) for the 1707 Act of Union that bound Scotland to England. In the House of Commons, Opposition MPs may like to remember that it was Anne who embraced the concept of a multi-party Parliament. Bookies and hat-makers would do well to reflect that it was Anne who introduced horse-racing at Ascot. Gardeners might linger over a delicate flower called 'Queen Anne's Lace'. Perhaps Anne's reign will be remembered as an important period in the arts and sciences; Swift, Defoe and Pope flourished; John Vanbrugh and Christopher Wren built their finest architecture; and Sir Isaac Newton was honoured by the Queen. But, finally, perhaps it will always be the memory of her almost lifelong devotion to one woman which will outlive the others. One afternoon in March 1967, the playwright Joe Orton (no stranger himself to camp nuances) was leafing through the *Encyclopaedia Britannica*. After reading the entry on Queen Anne, he wondered if Lewis Carroll had been influenced by her reign when writing *Alice in Wonderland*. 'The Queen and the Duchess seem reminiscent of Anne and the Duchess of Marlborough,' observed Orton.[11]

Sarah died in 1744, aged eighty-four, and the Churchills lie buried together in the chapel at Blenheim. Her tomb is marked with an ornate engraving. By contrast, Anne lies in front of the altar in Henry VII's chapel in Westminster Abbey, without any memorial. A statue of her stands in front of St Paul's Cathedral, but even this became a figure of fun, as yet another popular rhyme illustrates:

Brandy Nan
Now you're left in the lurch

27: Queen Anne and Sarah Churchill

Your face to the gin shops
Your back to the church

The organizers of Queen Victoria's Diamond Jubilee service in 1897, discovering that the statue severely hindered their plans, suggested that it should be temporarily moved – a proposal which was dismissed by the Queen.

After Anne's death, Sarah had made one last, desperate attempt to link her family to the Crown: she offered the Prince of Wales (later George II) £100,000 to marry her granddaughter, Lady Diana Spencer. He did not accept. It was to be more than two hundred and fifty years before her namesake and descendant fulfilled this family ambition – with the disastrous results now so well chronicled. In June 1993, the British yellow press was also full of headlines and pictures which told of the undignified arrest of Jamie Blandford, heir to the Marlborough fortune and Blenheim Palace. Young Jamie was dragged screaming and swearing from his London flat by police for failing to keep up maintenance payments for his estranged wife and child.

Given the fates of the latter-day Spencer-Churchills – Jamie Blandford's humiliating arrest and the emotional anguish and failed marriage of the former Diana Spencer – their clan might feel justified in thinking they are the victims of a Royal curse from beyond the grave, from 'Brandy Nan, left in the lurch' and reflect on the irony of their family motto: 'Faithful though unfortunate'.

Notes

1. David Green, *Sarah, Duchess of Marlborough* (London, Collins, 1967), p. 26.
2. Edward Gregg, *Queen Anne* (London, Ark, 1984), p. 44.
3. Beatrice Curtis Brown, *The Letters of Queen Anne* (London, Cassell, 1935), May 1692.
4. David Green, *Queen Anne* (London, Collins, 1970), p. 116.
5. Curtis Brown, *Letters*, October 1702, p. 67.
6. *Ibid.*
7. *Ibid.*, p. 212.
8. R. Scott Stevenson, *Famous Illnesses in History* (London, Eyre & Spottiswoode, 1962), p. 219.

9.   Gregg, *Queen Anne*, p. 276.

10.   A. L. Rowse, *The Early Churchills* (London, Macmillan, 1956), p. 322.

11.   John Lahr (ed.), *The Orton Diaries* (London, Methuen, 1986), p. 128.

Mercedes De Acosta: 'The Spanish Lothario'

IN a letter to Anita Loos in 1960, Alice B. Toklas recalled how a friend had commented, 'You can't dispose of Mercedes lightly – she has had the two most important women in the US – Greta Garbo and Marlene Dietrich.'[1] There are, undoubtedly, worse reasons for claiming a place in lesbian history – indeed, the consummate ease with which Judy Nelson fled into the arms of Rita Mae Brown after she had been unceremoniously dumped by Martina Navratilova suggests that this history lesson was not lost on at least one latter-day lesbian. It is amusing to imagine, had Mercedes De Acosta been born fifty years later, who might have been included on her list of conquests: Martina? Madonna? k. d. lang? Maybe even second-tier members of the Royal Family? The 'Spanish Lothario' was just that kind of gal – her life and her loves were global, all-encapsulating and conducted with a religious intensity that did credit to her early Catholicism and her later adoption of Eastern philosophies.

Mercedes De Acosta was born in Paris in 1900, raised in New York, but never considered herself, or was described, as anything other than Spanish. She was the eighth and last child in a family of three boys and five girls, the offspring of Micaela and Ricardo De Acosta – Castilian Spaniards who, after a series of bizarre, barely credible quirks of fate, had ended up in New York.

According to De Acosta, Micaela had been orphaned at an early age when her mother, heiress to the family fortune, died on board a ship in the Bay of Biscay. She had been in hot pursuit of an uncle who had poisoned her husband and then fled to France with the family inheritance. After her death, the young Micaela was raised by a family friend in Madrid. When she was fourteen her villainous great-uncle died and it was disclosed that most of the stolen fortune had ended up in American investments. This set off a lengthy legal battle to regain the money, eventually winding up in the U.S. Supreme Court.

Ricardo De Acosta was born in Cuba, where his father worked on the plantations, but the family moved back to Madrid after a few years. They returned to Cuba when Ricardo was a teenager, but he was forced to flee the island after taking part in an ill-advised student-based revolution. He settled in New York, where he worked in a succession of menial jobs. Eventually he landed a job on a Spanish newspaper, where he was paid a dollar a day to write editorials and poetry. His fortunes turned, though, when he started work for a shipping line that ran between New York and the West Indies. He met Micaela when she was sixteen and fresh from winning her inheritance of a million dollars. He persuaded her to stay in America and marry him.

The young couple lived on fashionable 47th Street in New York; their neighbours included Theodore Roosevelt and the actress Maude Adams, the first stage 'Peter Pan'. The De Acosta children were raised in an atmosphere of opulence, privilege and culture. They had their own nurses and rode ponies on the vast estates of other wealthy New York families. The household boasted a cook, a butler and two other servants who had been with their mother since her wedding day.

Although she was proud of her Castilian heritage, in later years Mercedes said she regretted having too Spanish a character because 'it imposes upon the consciousness a far too tragic sense of life'.[2] You can see her point: her father committed suicide by throwing himself off a cliff; her eldest brother, Joaquim, died at fifteen when he was accidentally hit on the head with a baseball bat; and her youngest brother, Enrique, gassed himself in his bedroom and was discovered by Mercedes herself.

Her eldest sister, Rita, was her mother's favourite, even after her marriage to a Protestant traumatized the staunchly Catholic matriarch. The two spoke nothing but Spanish to each other. Mercedes, by contrast, had little in common with her mother – the youngest De Acosta was an early and avid reader, who wrote poetry and was interested in the arts and science, while her mother considered all art, except music, 'trash'. Her children regularly attended the opera and theatre but, since Micaela did not approve, they often had to buy the cheapest tickets out of their weekly allowances.

The De Acostas were very much part of New York's fashionable, affluent society, both attending and hosting endless lavish dinners and parties. The family would have frequent holidays in Europe; every summer, they rented a house in Normandy, in the small, exclusive resort of Houlgate. A sulking Mercedes would be crammed into stiff party frocks and ribbons and dragged to the *Bal d'Enfants* where the wealthy showed off their children. Here, she had to dance with an endless string of little boys, each of whom she later remembered, 'could not lead me as well as I could have him'.[3] In Paris, the ten-year-old was introduced to the likes of Sarah Bernhardt, Rodin and Queen Marie of Romania. She became familiar with the works of the great Dutch painters and saw her first bullfight in Madrid – an event which precipitated her subsequent conversion to vegetarianism.

In the great tradition of little tomboys who grow up into big tomboys, Mercedes did not play with dolls. Instead, her favourite toy was a white rocking horse in whose stirrups she used to stand and 'lasso everything in sight'[4] – no great surprise, really, given how efficiently she hauled in lovers in later years.

Her first school was a day convent in New York, where she soon became involved in a doomed passion. Her form teacher, Sister Isabel, was in love with another nun, Sister Clara, and the pair enlisted Mercedes as their go-between, to deliver their love notes and act as look-out during their brief trysts. In *Here Lies the Heart* she made it perfectly clear that she knew what was going on and was in total sympathy with the nuns. Inevitably, the affair was discovered and Sister Clara was packed off to China for her penance. Their go-between witnessed the heartbreaking farewell and promptly had a fit of hysteria, weeping, bashing her head against the wall and setting off the fire alarm – not to mention alarm bells with her mother, who decided a change of convent might be advisable.

But the melancholia-inclined child was no happier at a boarding school in New Jersey, where she went on hunger strike and refused to speak, or at another convent in New York. Matters were made worse by her father's suicide: the family's extravagant standard of living suddenly plummeted and their house was sold, although they were not exactly penniless and were merely forced to move to a smaller home on Madison Avenue. When Enrique followed his father's example, it left Mercedes as the only child still living with her mother, both deeply traumatized by his death. They went on an extended visit to France but were forced to cut short the trip when war broke out in 1914, returning to live in rural Southampton, at the far end of Long Island.

De Acosta spent the war years finishing her erratic formal education, while keeping up her interests in the arts and literature. Once America became involved in the war, she trained as a nurse's aide at New York's Presbyterian Hospital and spent her evenings and early mornings writing poetry and the beginnings of a novel. During these years, she also met idols such as Ivor Novello, Isadora Duncan and the infamous actress Alla Nazimova.

De Acosta became involved in the struggle for women's rights, canvassing the burghers of Southampton on their doorsteps. More significantly, she began her long-term fascination with Eastern mysticism and religions, initially discovering the *Bhagavad-Gita*, and embarking on the gradual discarding of her Catholicism. In 1918, she met Hope Williams, an aspiring actress, at a party and began a relationship that would involve her further in the theatre. She set out to find a producer who would stage a musical comedy that could star Hope in the leading role and give her fledgling career a kick-start. The subsequent show, *What's Next?*, was staged semi-professionally and cast Hope as a Swedish servant called (what else?) Brunhilde.

Meanwhile, De Acosta was starting to achieve some success of her own. She took her first novel, *Wind Chaff*, and a volume of prose poetry, *Moods*, to Moffat and Yard. They were published in 1919. She also struck up a fruitful working relationship with Harriet Monroe, editor of the Chicago-based *Poetry* magazine, who published her poems until 1931. She was also spending more and more time on her mystic and religious studies. At this time, however, her mother began pressuring her to marry, and soon a suitable candidate appeared. She had met Abram Poole, a little-known painter, in the spring of 1919 and he quickly proposed marriage. Despite his attraction for the highly unusual De Acosta, and his occupation as a creator of what her mother called 'trash', he was a deeply conventional man, preoccupied with other people's opinions of him and always seeking their approval. When De Acosta told him she would not take his surname after the marriage, he could only worry about what 'they' would think. This odd couple were married on 11 May 1920, in her mother's apartment. One guest was obviously wise to the situation: just before the ceremony, he whispered to the butch bride, 'You should never be married – you have ten minutes to change your mind.' She didn't.

Incredibly, they remained technically married for fifteen years but the liaison was clearly a hollow shell. She spent her wedding night with her mother and, of her honeymoon in Chicago, she recalled that meeting up with Harriet Monroe was 'my happiest and most vivid experience during these weeks in Chicago'.[5] From then on, the couple hardly spent any time together and it is certain that Poole was the only man she ever had sex with. He hardly gets a mention in her memoirs and then it is entirely without any of the tenderness or passion afforded to the women in her life. Ludicrously, she later claimed to have been shocked when Poole asked her for a divorce so he could marry another woman. However, she agreed when it turned out to be a ploy to get her back to New York.

Her marriage appeared to have little effect on her lifestyle; she continued to travel and, in 1922, her best volume of poetry, *Streets and Shadows*, was published. Although her poetry was not technically outstanding, it was characterized by the De Acosta passion. There were several main themes which ran through her work: her love for different parts of New York – Manhattan, Fifth Avenue – and tributes to her mother, who died that year and whom she mourned deeply, as 'a rare flower of the old Spain'.[6] Another common theme was the cherishing and pursuit of freedom; birds featured often, their song likened to memories that live on for ever, even when the people or events have died or flown. She also showed a superficial social awareness in other poems. In 'For Rent' she observed the bitterness of the homeless camped outside countless empty properties; 'Leaning Out of Windows' deals with poverty again, this time of life in squalid rooms with torn wallpaper and the smell of greasy soup and greasy children, where the only escape for the weary and downtrodden parents is to look out of the window.

Many of her poems, though, dealt (inevitably) with lost loves. 'Rest' is an erotic ode to what is clearly a female lover; De Acosta delights in 'the boyishness of your slender figure' – nobody describes a man's body as 'boyish'. And in 'Goodbye on the Boat' she bids farewell to a lover about to embark on a long sea voyage and regrets not being able to kiss 'the way I wanted' – obviously because she could not kiss a woman lover passionately in front of the dockside crowd.

When her mother died, the distraught daughter locked herself away in her bedroom for days on end. She later poured her grief and sense of tragedy into a suitably dark play, *Jehanne D'Arc*. While writing this, she met Natacha Rambova, former lover of Alla Nazimova. The two of them must have found they had much in common: not only were they both obsessed with ancient religions, they had each entered into 'lavender' marriages – in Rambova's case, unconsummated wedlock with Rudolph Valentino.

In 1923, De Acosta's writing career received a boost when the celebrated stage actress, Eva Le Gallienne, starred in her play, *Botticelli*. The critics demolished it, but De Acosta later admitted that her hastily written, thin script had deserved no better. However, she must have done something right (possibly offstage), as Le Gallienne hired her to do some stage management work on her next show.

Le Gallienne was not the only drama queen that De Acosta was close to: she claimed to have been an intimate confidante of the Italian idol Eleanora Duse, even telling some cronies that she had been her lover. Duse certainly had her share of lesbian admirers, one of whom was the poet Amy Lowell, who befriended De Acosta and introduced her to the dubious delights of black cigars.

Le Gallienne, obviously unperturbed by her previous disastrous collaboration with De Acosta, agreed to star in *Jehanne* in Paris. It opened at the Porte St Martin Theatre in June 1926. It was a wildly expensive production: the theatre cost 7000 dollars a month, no fewer than 150 extras were hired for the crowd scenes and their stage shoes alone cost 500 dollars. It received mixed reviews – the French press mostly praised it but in America they only spoke highly of the set. However, it completed its run and author and star had a gay old time in Paris. After the performance, they would have supper at Chez Fischer, a trendy café, where the Russian-born singer Dora Stroeva would serenade diners in her deep voice, wearing a man's dinner jacket and short, slicked-back hair. In her memoirs, De Acosta remembered that the club was full of women wearing all manner of men's jackets, observing that it was a time when women would try to look masculine, and men feminine. 'Which after all', she noted, 'proves once again that there is nothing new under the sun.'[7] Quite.

On the boat back to New York, they met up with Noël Coward, who was on his way to open in *The Vortex* on Broadway. He observed that the disappointing production had left their moods swinging between 'intellectual gloom and feverish gaiety',[8] and that the pair dressed in nothing but black. On their return, Le Gallienne went on to establish her renowned Civic Repertory Theatre and she and De Acosta did not see each other again until the 1930s when they were both in Hollywood.

Mercedes saw Coward regularly during his New York trip, having supper with him on matinée days. Meanwhile, she wrote another play (unproduced), *The Dark Light*, and befriended the talented, alcoholic actress Jeanne Eagels. She accompanied Nazimova to Paris and, while there, found her old friend Isadora Duncan in a sorry state. The dancer had become too fond of the bottle, had driven most of her friends away and was penniless. De Acosta maintained that she persuaded Duncan to write her auto-biography to revive her fortunes.

On her return to New York, she wrote another play, *Jacob Slovak*, about the persecution of an elderly Jewish man in small-town America. When it opened in December 1926, some critics deemed it to be 'unrealistic' – a bitter irony, given what lay in store for Europe's Jews. Under the title *Prejudice*, it was given a one-off performance at the Arts Theatre in London in 1928, starring John Gielgud and Gwen Ffrangcon Davies. Gielgud played the lead role, one he found 'showy and dramatic' in a 'rather effective melo-drama'.[9]

In 1929 De Acosta's agent, Adrienne Morrison, secured her a commission with RKO Pictures to write a synopsis for the screen vamp, Pola Negri. The company were suitably impressed with her outline, called 'East River', and she was put under contract. And so Mercedes De Acosta got the Hollywood Call and headed west – a move that was to be a significant watershed in her life.

Once she arrived in Tinseltown, Negri showed her the social ropes, advising her which were the best parties to attend and which invitations to turn down. Her appearance and dress immediately caused a stir: her habitual attire of baggy white trousers did not go down well with the studio *apparatchiks*. 'You'll get a bad reputation if you dress this way out here,' she was warned.[10] Her monochrome appearance remained a talking point throughout her life. Maria Riva, Marlene Dietrich's daughter, thought De Acosta looked like 'a Spanish Dracula';[11] with her chalk-white face and jet-black hair and eyes. Clifton Webb always referred to her as 'Madame Dracula De Acosta'.[12] Tallulah Bankhead was scathing about De Acosta, likening her to 'a mouse dressed in a topcoat',[13] and Greta Garbo always referred to Mercedes as 'the little black and white friend'.[14]

Ah yes, Garbo. Greta. The Ice Queen. De Acosta had glimpsed her once in a hotel in 1922, but it was only when she made the move to Hollywood that they finally met. However, the two women, in their respective memoirs, told quite different stories about this first meeting. And so, for your delight and amusement, here are those synopses, together for the first time, in glorious rose-tinted Technicolor:

The Garbo Version

A shy, retiring Swedish film star lives on San Vicente Boulevard, in the Brentwood district. She becomes aware of a small, smartly dressed woman whom she observes passing her house frequently and staring at her. Mercedes De Acosta (for it is she) introduces herself as a screenwriter and declares that she wishes to share 'a great spiritual kinship'. Not surprisingly, Garbo fobs her off but is intrigued by the approach and makes enquiries among the Hollywood community, who speak complimentarily of De Acosta's writing, travelling and wardrobe. No one, it was said, had ever seen her twice in the same outfit. A few months later, Garbo receives an invitation to a De Acosta party; on the day, Garbo pleads illness, De Acosta swoops down with a bag of oranges and lemons, pledging to cure the stricken star of her cold. The De Acosta philosophy of combining a healthy diet, exercise, meditation and love appeals to Garbo, her resistance lowering by the minute. On subsequent visits, De Acosta extols the virtues of vegetarianism and meditation as the path to a world where same-sex love would be 'a form of prayer'. Garbo is more interested in De Acosta's butch attire – why does she dress like that? Easy: 'to attract other women', explains the veggie vamp to the screen goddess. The two women are next seen heading off for a 'honeymoon' holiday at Silver Lake. Cut, roll credits.

The De Acosta Version

Newly arrived scriptwriter De Acosta receives an invitation to have tea with colleague Salka Viertel at her Santa Monica home. Dressed in her usual natty white flannels, she is overwhelmed when she is introduced to screen goddess Greta Garbo. After the party, Viertel tells her that Garbo liked her – 'and she likes few people'.[15] Soon, the Viertels hold another party and invite both women. They dance and sing along to poignant tunes such as 'Daisy, You're Driving Me Crazy' and 'Goodnight Sweetheart'. Garbo sits in the garden with De Acosta, silent, watching the sunset. Soon, the two women are seen disappearing into it, heading towards Silver Lake. Cut, roll credits.

Well, at least the endings are the same.

The six weeks they spent together at Silver Lake were described in romanticized detail by De Acosta: 'six perfect weeks out of a lifetime ... I laughed more than ever before in my life and it was Greta who made me laugh'.[16] The starry-eyed lovers lived off simple food and drink, occasionally rowing across the lake to a lumber camp for provisions. They would walk in the Sierra Nevada mountains and swim naked in the icy waters of the 14-mile long lake itself. At the end of the holiday, Garbo did not want to return to Hollywood. When she did, she moved house to be nearer to De Acosta (she never lived with anyone). They rode and played tennis together often, had picnics on the beach at Malibu and went to bed early. Years later, Garbo allegedly recalled: 'Looking back, I can see that my relationship with her gave me not only new sexual experience and spiritual peace for a time, but above all the foundation on which to base [Queen Christina].'[17]

Garbo started to wear trousers in public, which led to one of her stranger headlines: 'Garbo in Pants!' She and De Acosta were photographed striding down Hollywood Boulevard similarly attired; the photocaption read, 'Innocent bystanders gasped in amazement'. De Acosta always found it a strange reaction, 'considering what walks down Hollywood Boulevard now'.[18] What *can* she have meant?

De Acosta's career with RKO was short-lived – something that may not have been unconnected with her personal life. However, Garbo brought her to the attention of Irving Thalberg, the diminutive and determined head of production at MGM and the inspiration for F. Scott Fitzgerald's *The Last Tycoon*. She presented a synopsis, 'Desperate', to Thalberg and as a result was put under contract. However, he soon discovered her script called for Garbo to dress as a man in one scene – De Acosta was carpeted. 'We've been building Garbo up for years as a great glamorous actress and now you come along and try to put her in pants ...',[19] he told her. That was par for the course for a Hollywood writer in those days.

In 1932, the Hollywood studios employed 354 full-time writers, with another 435 part-timers; by the mid-1930s it had risen to around a thousand. They came from a variety of backgrounds – some from the redundant vaudeville circuits, while others had written solely for the theatre. Yet more were recruited from the lowly paid news or features desks of regional newspapers and magazines. During the period 1929–30, Hollywood went on a mass recruitment drive from the literary set strewn up and down the East Coast, but few stayed longer than a couple of months. From this rich source, MGM also pulled the likes of Christopher Isherwood, Dorothy Parker, S. J. Perelman and Aldous Huxley.

For most, the working conditions lacked glamour: small buildings spilling over with thirty or forty writers, churning out everything from Westerns to romantic comedies, while outside on the sound stages or the exteriors on the back lots, anything from jungles to urban slums were recreated. Later, there was even a vast water tank, with inch-thick glass walls, where Esther Williams could dive without danger. Nathanael West, hired by Columbia for seven weeks, described the pressure-cooker atmosphere: 'All the writers sit in cells and the minute a typewriter stops someone pokes his head in the door to see if you are thinking.'[20]

Thalberg insisted that his house writers signed personal contacts forbidding them from any union membership. If they did not comply, they were out. Writers were hired by MGM on short-term contracts to work on a specific film, and were released once the script was finished. They were not treated well: many were not allowed onto the set of any film they had worked on and often they were not even invited to previews. A few were treated on a par with the stars whose dialogue they would be providing: P. G. Wodehouse, for example, was brought to Hollywood by MGM, paid 2,000 dollars a week and housed in the former residence of Norma Shearer. But generally, MGM was more interested in lavishing attention, cash and trimmings on its stars than on its writers and directors, and most scripts would have passed through the typewriters of half a dozen scribes before they were committed to celluloid.

Most writers who were employed on a script would receive no credit for their work. Whatever the writers produced could be scrapped, altered, retained indefinitely and credited to another writer. De Acosta's involvement with 'Rasputin' was typical of how the system worked. In 1934 Thalberg announced that MGM was to make a great picture featuring what was regarded then as Hollywood's Royal Family, the Barrymores: Lionel, John and Ethel. The film, said Thalberg, would be the story of Rasputin and his grisly death; Lionel would play the title role, Ethel the Tsarina and John the Russian Prince who was one of Rasputin's assassins. Because of Ethel Barrymore's stage commitments, the script had to be completed quickly and it was down to Mercedes De Acosta to come up with the first draft. Thalberg was underwhelmed: the script called for lots of naked women plus a number of orgies featuring the Russian Prince – and then more orgies. He insisted that the script should be more specific about the identity of the Prince – Alexis Youssoupoff. De Acosta argued that this would land MGM in hot water with the still-very-much-alive Prince and his wife. Thalberg was not convinced by her arguments and terminated her contract. A series of writers were called in to transform her first draft into something that would make it past the censors *and* be more forthcoming about who had killed Rasputin; eventually it was given over to accomplished scribe Charles MacArthur.

In his book, *Rasputin in Hollywood*, British lawyer Sir David Napley said that MacArthur's Academy Award-nominated script 'bore about as much relation to what occurred in Russia in 1916 as, to quote those two gentlemen, "the flowers that bloom in the spring" '.[21] The film was released as *Rasputin, the Mad Monk* (*Rasputin and the Empress* in America) and was promptly greeted with a libel suit – courtesy of Prince and Princess Youssoupoff.

By this time, Garbo's feelings towards De Acosta were starting to swing the other way (literally). By the spring of 1932 they were beginning to have rows and, at one point, Garbo left for New York, refusing to see De Acosta. That summer, she went on an extended trip to Sweden and De Acosta stayed in America, busy with the abortive 'Rasputin' script. She pined for Garbo but another suitor soon appeared: Marlene Dietrich. Again, there are different versions of how they met. De Acosta said that they first met when Cecil Beaton took Dietrich to the theatre. According to Maria Riva, her mother's introduction to Mercedes came during a party at Irving Thalberg's house, where Dietrich found De Acosta in the kitchen, sobbing because of Garbo's hot-and-cold behaviour towards her. She also told Riva that De Acosta was upset because, she claimed, Garbo's sexual swings and roundabouts had left her with gonorrhoea. Dietrich wrote to her estranged husband, Rudy Seiber, that she found De Acosta 'very attractive ... a relief from this narrow Hollywood mentality'.[22] In a subsequent letter, she repeated her attraction to De Acosta, voiced concern about her state of health and announced that she was going to cook her back to fitness.

In typical Dietrich fashion, De Acosta was soon taking daily delivery of enormous bouquets of flowers; she reciprocated by sending her 'Wonderful One' romantic notes several times a day, usually signed from her 'White Prince' or 'Raphael'. They spent many weekends together at Dietrich's rented beach house in Santa Monica. De Acosta claimed credit for introducing Dietrich to the sartorial style sported by her in the 1930s: white flannel trousers and silk shirts, cream polo-neck jumpers and berets, complete with short, boyish haircuts. However, Maria Riva disputed this, pointing out that this style was *de rigueur* for the tennis-playing set in Hollywood. True, but it is interesting that the snapshots De Acosta took of Garbo and Dietrich were invariably of them at their butchy best, in trousers or shorts (Garbo topless in some), and completely free of their 'Screen Goddess' personae so carefully cultivated by the studios.

De Acosta appears to have irritated Dietrich by assuming that her split with former lover and mentor Josef von Sternberg had been because of her. She put her foot in it even more when her frequent letters contained as much about her love for Garbo as her love for Dietrich, despite the obviously intense sexual side of their relationship. Before too long, Dietrich, typically, began an affair with co-star Brian Aherne and De Acosta's calls and visits were thwarted — her 'Wonderful One' was often 'not feeling well'. Apparently, she believed these excuses — or perhaps persuaded herself to believe them. The more desperate her attempts to keep Dietrich became, the more the situation deteriorated. Once, she offered to arrange for Dietrich to have any lover she named. Years later, Maria Riva waggishly wondered what De Acosta would have done if Dietrich had replied, 'Bring me Garbo!' However, Dietrich remained a good friend. In 1934, De Acosta had a serious car crash and required some facial plastic surgery. Dietrich rang her from Paris, moved her to a better hospital room and footed the bill.

Meanwhile, back at the fantasy factory, De Acosta laboured over a screen version of 'Joan of Arc' in which she envisaged Garbo as the star, but Garbo refused the role. Instead, she starred in *Camille* in 1936, a script for which De Acosta had also carried out some research. Shortly after this, Thalberg died and she was one of many swept out when the new brooms took over. She returned to her previous occupations: travelling and mysticism. She was introduced to the Indian guru, Sri Meher Baba, and went on yet another trip to Europe in the summer of 1938. During her train journey from Berlin to Poland, her luggage was removed and searched. She later discovered that she had been under surveillance by the Nazis because she was Spanish and suspected of being an anti-fascist loyalist.

Before she returned to America, she travelled to Meher Baba's ashram in Ahmadnagar. When the guru insisted that she remain there for five years, she moved on to the ultimate in spiritual leaders, the Bhagavan Maharishi in Tiruvannamalai. She spent days sitting at his feet awaiting enlightenment, which was not always forthcoming. 'What is death and what is birth?', she enquired, getting straight to the point. 'There is, in Reality, neither birth nor death' may not have been quite the enlightenment she was looking for.[23]

Still, she returned to Hollywood in the spring of 1939, a spiritually changed woman. It was De Acosta who introduced Garbo to the philosophies of Gayelord Hauser, an exponent of natural medicine and health foods. She became interested for a while, although she suspected that De Acosta was trying to get her to endorse Hauser publicly. However, this did not prevent her from endorsing him in private for a few years, during which time she retired from films. Garbo's suspicions were not entirely dishonour-able: during their long association, De Acosta was not averse to effecting introductions between Garbo and starstruck young hopefuls. In the mid-1950s, she invited Andy Warhol to join them on a picnic. The young artist, then working in advertising, could not believe his luck: he considered De Acosta herself to be the height of elegance, envying her European footwear and even her shoe-trees which were carved by a violin-maker. He was so much in awe of Garbo that he could not bring himself to speak to her, and instead drew her a butterfly on a napkin which she absentmindedly threw away at the end of the day. However, De Acosta loyally refused to use her influence with Garbo when numerous producers and directors tried to coax the star out of the retirement that began in 1941.

By that time, America was at war in Europe and De Acosta had moved back to New York, where she became editor of an Office of War Information propaganda magazine called *Victory*. Once the war was over, she got a job in Paris writing articles for a syndicated newspaper, and set up house with an American woman,

Poppy Kirk (real name, Maria Annunziata Sartori). Kirk had enjoyed a similar cosmopolitan upbringing and De Acosta found her 'deliciously unique'.[24] They divided their time between an apartment in Paris and a farmhouse in Normandy.

By the early 1950s, however, life was a little gloomier. Many old friends were dead, some by suicide, others from lengthy illnesses, and her own health had become erratic. When she returned to New York in 1952, she and Poppy went their separate ways. She was still able to afford to travel regularly and in style. Alice B. Toklas recalled meeting her on a bus in Paris in the autumn of 1951: 'she has become so very bourgeois looking and comfortably middle aged'.[25] She was there with Beaton and Garbo, then rumoured to be about to marry – a curious trio, to say the least. Beaton had met De Acosta in 1929 in New York while on a photographic assignment for *Vogue*. Initially, Beaton was attracted to her and later confessed in his diaries that he would have liked to go to bed with her – perhaps her typically butch attire further confused the man who loathed his own homosexuality.

Garbo seemed oblivious to any suffering Beaton's constant presence caused De Acosta, but Beaton himself was more sensitive to the situation. For example, in 1947, the three of them spent Christmas Day together at Mercedes's apartment. Beaton's presence was a surprise to De Acosta; Garbo merely warned her to lay on another plate for 'an extra lost soul'. Not surprisingly, the atmosphere was rather tense and muted, but Garbo took over the proceedings and put on an amusing impromptu performance of song and poetry. It was a curious programme: the hymn of the Swedish Salvation Army and 'Nobody Knows the Troubles I've Seen But Jesus' were highlights. She also put on a performance in the kitchen, whipping up ham and eggs for the assembled guests, and then supervised the present distribution. An ill-at-ease Mercedes made a foolish attempt to score Brownie points over the other guests, constantly alluding to some happy episode or other that she and Garbo had shared. She scored no points with Garbo herself for this.

A few weeks before this, Garbo and Beaton had been discussing their mutual friend. Garbo said that De Acosta was alone, unpopular and miserable, and complained that she had harmed her

(Garbo) by gossiping and vulgarity – obviously, De Acosta's openness did not sit well with the Swedish swinger. She even thought it was vulgar for De Acosta to ask Beaton if he and Garbo were having an affair.

Beaton disliked the effect that Garbo had on her: De Acosta became tactless and silly. When with others, Beaton found her fascinating and amusing. De Acosta admitted to Marlene Dietrich that her feelings towards Garbo were confused and so, therefore, was her behaviour. Her head, she said, told her that the real Garbo was 'a Swedish servant girl with a face touched by God',[26] and admitted that the person she loved was the Garbo that her emotions had created. She also admitted to Beaton that she found her great friend to be 'a complex mixture of greatness and pettiness'.[27]

Garbo continued to blow hot and cold with her. By the winter of 1958, having not contacted De Acosta for a year, she suddenly turned up at her apartment in floods of tears, wailing that she was lost, frightened and had no one to look after her. De Acosta, quite fairly, replied that Garbo did not want anyone to look after her – she would not even let De Acosta have her telephone number.

But the final rupture occurred in April 1960 when De Acosta published her memoirs, *Here Lies the Heart*. Toklas was gushing in her response to them. In a letter to the 'dearest most wonderful – surprising and adorable of women', she declared the book 'a delight' and claimed it left her 'breathless ... ravished',[28] and was full of praise for the portraits of Garbo and Dietrich. However, not all of De Acosta's friends and acquaintances were so impressed with her revelations about them. Singer Libby Holman was amused by De Acosta's account of how she had visited a White Russian fortune-teller, who supposedly predicted Holman's subsequent marriage to Camel cigarette heir Zachary Smith Reynolds, and his mysterious death from gun wounds. She told friends that De Acosta had written a book called 'Here Lies the Heart – and Lies and Lies and Lies'.

For Garbo, it was the last straw: De Acosta was out, once and for all. One observer noted, 'If you are Garbo's friend and would remain so, you've got to take the oath of silence.'[29] Although De Acosta admitted in her book that she had misgivings in disclosing so many intimate details of her relationship with Garbo, it was against her nature to cover up or lie. Her frank and forthright autobiography cost her her friendship with Garbo and was her last real claim to fame. In it, she concluded, 'despite the many years behind me, I feel now as if I am only beginning life'.[30]

However, her optimism can only have been skin-deep. All her life, she had been plagued by migraines and, in 1961, underwent a series of brain operations. She never fully recovered and, in 1966, knowing how ill she was, Cecil Beaton tried to bring about a reconciliation with Garbo. He had always felt that Garbo had treated De Acosta unfairly and cruelly and had tried to get her to visit her at the time of the operations. However, although she was apparently very upset at De Acosta's physical decline, she made no attempt to contact her. De Acosta died in 1968, to the end unforgiven for her honesty.

Her uncompromising expression of her sexuality was almost certainly responsible for the obstacles she encountered in her career. It is true that the erratic treatment she received was dished out by studios to many writers, but her openness and, partly, her influence over a major 'property' like Garbo would have made her particularly vulnerable to dismissal or, more insidiously, lack of employment on the flimsiest of grounds. Such openness must have been alarming to all the residents of Hollywood's overcrowded closet and, even now, such a refusal to cover up would be admirable, let alone in the 1920s and 1930s.

Apart from her open sexuality, her lifestyle and beliefs were those of a grand old hippy – albeit a wealthy one. Her vegetarianism, her interests in alternative spirituality and non-Western religions and her espousal of liberal politics would not have been out of place in the 1960s or early 1970s.

Of course, her wealthy, cosmopolitan background gave her an enviable start in life. Even as a child she was acquainted (and at ease) with major figures in the arts and high society, who were to form the basis of a useful network of contacts. From this came her early adventures in the theatre and, consequently, her emigration to Hollywood and the relationship with the most important figure in her life: Garbo.

It is a certainty that her Spanish passion would have risen

beyond boiling point if she had known that she was to be remembered, not for what she committed to paper sheets, but for what (and more importantly, who) she did under cotton ones. Then again, history has always had its share of Great Lovers and Mercedes De Acosta is right up there with the best of them. She was just that kind of gal.

Notes

1. Edward Burns (ed.), *Staying on Alone: Letters of Alice B. Toklas* (New York, Vintage, 1975), p. 383.
2. Mercedes De Acosta, *Here Lies the Heart* (London, André Deutsch, 1960), p. 1.
3. De Acosta, *The Heart*, p. 31.
4. *Ibid*, p. 31.
5. *Ibid*, p. 116.
6. Mercedes De Acosta, *Streets and Shadows* (New York, Longmans, 1922), p. 32.
7. De Acosta, *The Heart*, p. 162.
8. Noël Coward, *Present Indicative* (London, Heinemann, 1937), p. 254.
9. John Gielgud, *Early Stages* (London, Macmillan, 1939), p. 112.
10. De Acosta, *The Heart*, p. 229.
11. Maria Riva, *Marlene Dietrich* (London, Bloomsbury, 1992), p. 154.
12. *Ibid*., p. 411.
13. Jon Bradshaw, *Dreams That Money Can Buy* (London, Cape, 1985), p. 84.
14. Cecil Beaton, *Diaries 1944–48* (London, Weidenfeld & Nicolson, 1972), p. 172.
15. De Acosta, *The Heart*, p. 214.
16. *Ibid*, p. 226.
17. Antoni Gronowicz, *Garbo: Her Story* (London, Simon & Schuster, 1990), p. 316.
18. De Acosta, *The Heart*, p. 229.
19. *Ibid*.
20. Ian Hamilton, *Writers in Hollywood* (London, Heinemann, 1990), p. 205.
21. Sir David Napley, *Rasputin in Hollywood* (London, Weidenfeld & Nicolson, 1990), p. 66.
22. Riva, *Dietrich*, p. 154.
23. De Acosta, *The Heart*, p. 299.
24. *Ibid*, p. 345.

25. Burns, *Staying on Alone*, p. 247.
26. Riva, *Dietrich*, p. 169.
27. Hugo Vickers, *Cecil Beaton* (London, Weidenfeld & Nicolson, 1985), p. 348.
28. Burns, *Staying on Alone*, p. 380.
29. F. Sands and S. Broman, *The Divine Garbo*, p. 227.
30. De Acosta, *The Heart*, p. 356.

Edy Craig and 'The Boys'

THE children of famous – even legendary – parents have little choice in life: they can either beat 'em or join 'em – by becoming part of the parents' fame and fortune as one of their courtiers, consorts or handservants. Of course, when neither of these two choices suits, and the offspring have been chewed up and spat out by the machinery of fame, there is a third option: getting even – the 'Mommie Dearest' syndrome. After Joan Crawford died without leaving a penny to her two eldest adopted children, her daughter, Christina, published her own account of 'life with mother'. The book, which at one point was selling 10,000 copies a day in America and was described by its author as 'a very sad love story', quickly became a byword to replace the old maxim that 'revenge is a dish best served cold'. Crawford had now rewritten it – it was a dish best served when the *body* is cold.

It opened the floodgates, and soon the lifestyles of the rich and famous were fair game for exposés by their disillusioned daughters. Some of them could not even wait until the bodies were cold: in 1985, Bette Davis, Joan Crawford's arch-rival, was recovering from cancer and a stroke when her daughter, Barbara, published *My Mother's Keeper*, chock-full of tales of drunkenness and domestic turmoil. Lana Turner's daughter, Cheryl Crane, spilled the beans about how she came to shoot one of her mother's lovers. At least Maria Riva, the only child of Marlene Dietrich, waited until her mother was dead before adding her two cents' worth (or, to be precise, £25-worth) by publishing her own version of life with 'Mutti'. Unfortunately for the perpetrators of these vicious tomes, the mud they threw at their mothers, though it stuck to the targets, soiled them for ever as well. What will they ever be remembered for except those books and their bitterness?

The daughter of another legendary actress could have told them a thing or two. Like Christina Crawford, she had once tried to follow in her mother's footsteps but, anticipating the futility of that, she opted out of acting. She subsequently devoted most of her early adult life to her mother's career, not leaving home until she was thirty. Even after carving a separate professional niche for herself, she and her life partner still spent many years embarking on projects in her mother's name. It would appear that Edy Craig, daughter of Ellen Terry, arguably one of the greatest stage actresses in the history of British theatre, learned at an early age just what the options were – and made her choice accordingly.

Edith Ailsa Geraldine Craig was born on 9 December 1869 at Gusterwoods Common, Hertfordshire, the eldest child of Ellen Terry and the architect and archaeologist Edward Godwin. Her younger brother, Edward (Ted) Gordon Craig, was later to find fame as a theatre designer and director. She was named Ailsa Craig after the famous Scottish rock and kept it as her stage name. Godwin was the great love of Ellen Terry's life, after a disastrous marriage at seventeen to the painter G. F. Watts, thirty years her senior. When she ran off with Godwin in 1869, she abandoned her stage career, resuming it when they parted six years later. The couple never married and the children barely got to know their father, something they came to resent. Ellen's second husband, Charles Kelly, and her stage partner Henry Irving were adequate substitute father-figures, but the children were not easy to handle. Brought up in the rarefied, slightly histrionic atmosphere that surrounded the most celebrated actress of her time, they nonetheless suffered from the social stigma of being born out of wedlock – though it is fair to say that, had their mother not been an actress, the stigmatization would have been far worse.

Ellen fluctuated from spoiling them to being over-strict. Her children were not allowed to read 'rubbishy picture books' and were only allowed to play with wooden toys. If friends gave them gifts deemed to be inappropriate, the offending objects were burned. Japanese prints adorned the nursery walls and the children had pet ponies and goats to play with. They spent their weekends in their mother's cottage at Hampton Court, where they would 'perform' plays on the garden lawn. The first theatre the young Edy saw was not one of her mother's performances but a circus. Unimpressed by what she saw, the young Edy ordered her mother to take her home.

Edy had a close, if tempestuous, relationship with her brother. They would call each other 'Miss Edy' and 'Master Teddy'; if Ted cried, his robust sister would hit him on the head with a wooden spoon, exhorting him 'to be a woman'.

Ellen Terry kept all her children's drawings from their schooldays. In her memoirs, she maintained that she had never put pressure on her children to emulate her success. She said their achievements 'have mattered very little. So long as they were not lazy, I have always felt I could forgive them anything'.[1]

Edy was fortunate enough to be educated at two radical schools: the first, a co-educational establishment in Earl's Court, run by a Mrs Cole; the second, in Gloucestershire and run by her sister, Mrs Malleson, who was a pioneer suffragette. After leaving school, Edy seemed set for a musical career. She studied first at the Royal Academy of Music in London and then went to Berlin to train as a pianist. This was cut short at twenty-one with the onset of chronic rheumatism, an ailment that would plague her all her life. Instead, she became a member of Irving's company at the Lyceum Theatre and for the next decade played a number of small parts in various productions. But, with her mother at the height of her glory, it was impossible for Edy to make any significant impact. George Bernard Shaw was given to remark that she was too clever for her profession.

It gradually became clear that, if her diverse talents could not be utilized on the stage, they could be used elsewhere. Her flair for creating costumes was noticed when Irving asked her to work on *Robespierre* in April 1899. Encouraged by this success, she set up her own theatrical costumier business near Covent Garden, with a little financial backing from her mother.

While Edy decided to remain living and working with her mother, her brother left home early, married young and went to Europe to establish his career away from the Terry name and legend. Ellen, for her part, always bailed him out when he was in debt and took care of his children when he neglected them. Her relationship with her daughter was close but complex; Edy gave her enormous practical and emotional support and Ellen would tell her how wonderful she was, while at the same time complaining about her to others. When they were with company, Edy was treated as one of the entourage by Ellen and not singled out for any special attention.

The axis of their relationship tilted away from Ellen after 1899, when Christopher St John entered Edy's life. Known as 'Chris', she was born Christabel Marshall in 1878, changing her name when she converted to Catholicism. Along with many young women, she had become an Ellen Terry devotee; conversion to this faith took place after a performance of *Ravenswood* at the Princes Theatre, Bristol. Like other Terry worshippers, Chris sent the actress flowers, presents and letters, some of which received brief replies. They did not meet until 1896, at Ellen's invitation, in her dressing-room at the Lyceum before a performance of *King Arthur*.

Edy always maintained she had no recollection of Chris at that time – and why would she? Her mother's dressing-room was always full of star-struck fans flapping around her mother like a flock of gulls. The official date of their meeting was in 1899. By then, Chris had graduated from Oxford and was working as a secretary and journalist and writing a novel in her spare time. After sending a poem to Ellen, she was again summoned for an audience, this time at the Grand Theatre, Fulham. Edy was given the task of looking after her – a not unfamiliar duty. She was busy mending a glove when Chris was brought to her dressing-room and forgot to put it down before they shook hands. The needle stuck in Chris's hand – or, as she described it, 'Cupid's dart, for I loved Edy from that moment'.[2] Despite being irritated by most of her mother's admirers (and, perhaps, a bit jealous), Edy later told Chris that she had taken to her instantly. The newcomer was invited back to the Terry home for a curious supper of grilled kidneys, rice pudding and mocha coffee. Edy and Chris arranged a lunch date for the next day, during which Chris was able to make a careful appraisal of the tall, dark and handsome new friend, who had a slight lisp. Chris herself had rather bulbous features, a slight limp and also had to contend with a cleft palate with gave her a speech impediment. However, it was the start of a lifelong, if not beautiful, relationship.

In the autumn of 1899, Ellen Terry and Henry Irving left for a tour of America and, with Ellen's approval, Edy and Chris set up home together in an elegant house in Smith Square, where they were to live for the next six years. Friends nicknamed them 'The Squares'. Chris was working in the India Office of the government, and she and Edy would often meet for picnic lunches in St James's Park. Their home was messy and chaotic; the telephone rang constantly and they rarely bothered to do any washing-up or cleaning. They ate out most of the time, usually at Gourmets Restaurant.

There has always been speculation about whether Ellen Terry recognized the nature of Edy and Chris's relationship. It is curious that she was happy to give her blessing to the pair when they first moved in together yet, before and after, whenever a man showed interest in Edy, Ellen reacted with hostility and concern. For instance, when Edy was on tour with her in 1895, she became infatuated with the painter Joe Evans, who was then married. Ellen promptly stepped in and nipped the affair in the bud.

Although she initially approved of Edy moving in with Chris, she had changed her mind by the time she returned from America, and accused Chris of luring her daughter away from the family home. Eventually she overcame her jealousy and came to regard Chris as part of the family. Chris later used this period in her relations with both Edy and Ellen as the basis for her novel, *Hungerheart*, published in 1915. In it, the mother Louise is jealous of her daughter Sally leaving home. In a telling conclusion, the 'Chris' figure is accepted by Louise and, from then on, becomes 'the willing slave of both mother and daughter'.[3]

But, in 1903, the 'willing slave' was faced with a major crisis in her relationship. Edy claimed to have fallen in love with Martin Shaw, one of her brother's friends. Shaw wanted to marry her, whereupon Chris tried to kill herself by swallowing a bottle of cocaine lotion prescribed for earache. Edy nursed her back to health and the relationship with Shaw cooled. Ellen's sympathies lay with Chris, and the wronged lover herself took revenge on Shaw by writing him into *Hungerheart* as 'Robin', an ugly, unattractive character (Shaw did have a facial disfigurement). In her own reminiscences of these first years with Edy, Chris merely referred to this time as 'near to being a tragedy' – a time which, apparently, they never discussed again.

Edy and her brother remained close but their relationship became strained after they tried working together at the Imperial Theatre in 1903, under Ellen's management. Edy supervised the costumes while Ted designed and directed, but the shows they produced together failed and Ted subsequently went to live and work abroad. That same year, Ellen Terry bought Smallhythe Place, a cottage and several smaller buildings near the Kent coast, which she had had her heart set on for years. Edy and Chris were given the adjacent Priest's House, a cottage a hundred yards from the main house. By now, Chris had become a fully integrated member of the Terry court, occasionally accompanying her on tour and ghosting her memoirs.

Meanwhile, Edy's costume business was foundering, but she had already begun to turn her talents towards producing. By 1909, she and Chris had become involved in the struggle for women's suffrage and made friends with the writer and campaigner, Cicely Hamilton, perhaps best-known to most people as the author of the lyrics for the suffragettes' anthem, *March of the Women*, composed by Ethel Smyth. Cicely Hamilton thought that it was inevitable, given a background where her mother's career was so important, that Edy should become a feminist. Edy was, however, less interested in the development of women in parliamentary politics and more an advocate of radical direct action. She was a member of the Women's Freedom League, many of whose members ended up in Holloway Prison, and also of the Actresses Franchise League, which organized fund-raising shows. When she and Chris moved to their new home in Bedford Street, it became a 'safe house' for suffragettes, hiding from the police or just released from prison. Chris took a more active part in the cause, distributing leaflets, taking part in demonstrations, heckling politicians, chalking 'Votes For Women' on the pavement and getting arrested for seizing a police horse's bridle.

Cicely and Chris co-wrote a one-act comedy called *How the Vote Was Won*, which was staged as a benefit for the Women Writers' Suffrage League. As a result of this collaboration, Edy asked Cicely to write a pageant for her on the theme of great women in history. Edy put forward plenty of suggestions for who should be included and the music that should go with them. The character of 'Woman' argued her case for equality and justice with the male figure, 'Prejudice'. *A Pageant of Great Women* was first produced at London's Scala Theatre, with a cast of nearly forty actresses. Edy herself played Rosa Bonheur, complete with palette and painter's smock, and entered to thunderous applause. She was to appear as Bonheur in a number of pageants over the years.

Edy's pageants became famous and were often staged in aid of charitable causes. In the early 1920s she produced one on the lives of famous saints. Gladys Cooper was St George, Sybil Thorndike played St Joan, Edy and Chris contented themselves with playing monks, while Edy's cousin, John Gielgud, appeared as a humble shepherd. Dame May Whitty, who had once been Edy's understudy, staged a pageant written by Chris about the history of theatre from early Greece onwards. Edy, as usual, took charge, rustling up the necessary costumes and staging the show at the Royal Albert Hall.

In 1911 Edy founded the Pioneer Players; Ellen Terry was president, Edy was director and Chris was secretary. Apart from two men on the advisory committee, all the other positions in the company were filled by women. Over the next ten years, they produced around a hundred and fifty plays in small London theatres, on Sundays only, and with actors and actresses who mostly remained unpaid. The production costs were covered by subscribers, who paid annual fees (on a sliding scale) which allowed them seats for all performances.

The aim of the Players was 'to present the type of play which is known as "the play of ideas" and particularly that variety which deals with current ideas, social, political and moral'.[4] For the times, the Players were a radical departure in British theatre. The shows had a strong feminist slant and the audiences were nearly always 99 per cent female. They opened on 8 May 1911 at the Kingsway Theatre with a triple bill of plays: Cicely Hamilton's *Jack and Jill and a Friend*, *In the Workhouse* by Margaret Wynne Nevinson and another collaboration between Chris and Cecily called *The First Actress*. Later, they staged *Mrs Warren's Profession*, a play about attitudes towards prostitution by George Bernard Shaw, which had been banned; and *Macrena*, a play by Chris about a ninth-century nun in Russia who dies rather than renounce her faith. *The Surprise of His Life*, a play about a woman who refuses to marry the man whose child she is expecting, had the press in an uproar. Despite their successes, the Pioneer Players were always strapped for cash. Edy herself was paid nothing for the first six years, and rehearsals and administrative work often took place in her London flat.

One of the women involved in designing sets for the Pioneer Players was Clare Atwood, known as 'Tony', a successful painter in her own right. Born in 1866, she had exhibited at the Royal Academy and was one of a few select artists to be officially commissioned during the First World War. She subsequently painted many portraits of the Terry family. We do not know whether Tony was as instantly smitten with Edy as Chris had been but, for her part, Edy obviously knew a good thing when she saw it. In 1916, she asked Tony if she would like to live with her and Chris – with the proviso that 'if Chris does not like your being here, and feels you are interfering with our friendship, out you go!'[5] But Chris had no such objections and the three of them lived together, in London and Smallhythe, until Edy's death.

This *ménage à trois* worked better than anyone could have reasonably expected. Chris herself later wrote of Tony, 'I cannot write that name without giving thanks to the divinity that shapes our ends for having brought Tony into our lives.' Vita Sackville-West also admired Tony for her soothing influence and droll sense of humour: 'Tony the reticent is perhaps the most secretive character of the whole encampment', she observed.[6] Of the three, Tony, by common consensus, had the sweetest, most tactful personality, whereas Edy, though talented and energetic, lacked charm. The combination of her dominant personality and Chris's stubbornness and rather jealous nature made for a certain unpredictability in the household, with Tony often serving as the peacekeeper. Tony was nicknamed 'The Brat' and Chris was 'Master Baby'. There are no prizes for guessing who the overall 'Master' was.

Chris did most of the gardening but they all took turns in cooking, and gave frequent tea parties in the flat in Bedford Street.

In the country, they gardened, had the occasional hop-picking excursion, and went for rides in Edy's car, nicknamed 'Belinda', driven by their gardener and handyman. Edy, of course, sat up front.

Perhaps the secret of their success was that, despite living together in London and Smallhythe, they did not always spend a great deal of time together because of their separate work commitments, even though they sometimes collaborated on projects and were always supportive of each other's work. But Chris's philosophy seemed, in this instance, to be correct: 'It is not how often people meet, but what happens when they meet which is the important thing in human relationships.'[7]

Once Edy had made the transition from acting to producing, her extensive stage experience paid off and she impressed many with her practical knowledge of scenery and lighting design; she was even able to select and arrange the music for shows. A reviewer in the *Arts Gazette* wrote in 1920, 'I have no hesitation in saying that Miss Craig has proved that she is second to none of the producers in this country, that she promises to vie with the great producers abroad ... she inspired the actors.'[8] However, despite such success, the West End theatrical establishment snubbed her, even though a number of influential figures lobbied hard for her to be appointed to the vacant position of stage-director at the Old Vic. Lilian Baylis, the fearsome manager of both the Old Vic and Sadler's Wells, categorically dismissed any suggestion that Edy should work there: 'We don't want another woman here. And anyway we don't want Edy. She would upset the staff.'[9] Presumably the hallowed walls of that revered theatre were not big enough for the both of them. It is also possible that Edy's unconventional and open (even for the theatre) personal life did not endear her to everyone.

John Gielgud thought Edy suffered because she lived at a time when women were largely kept out of important, influential roles in the theatre – except, of course, as actresses. It is interesting to speculate how she might have fared had she been born forty or fifty years later. It is not hard to envisage her as the doyenne of middle-class, rural, community-based theatre – a strange cross between Joan Littlewood, Ann Jellicoe (director of many shows involving local people in southern England) and 'Mapp and Lucia'.

Although Edy worked as assistant producer at the small Everyman Theatre in Hampstead and as stage-director at the Leeds Art Theatre, she longed for a theatre (rather than a room) of her own. Ironically, it was only when her mother died in 1928 that she got one.

Ellen Terry died at Smallhythe in July 1928. Edy was devastated: outside her bedroom, Chris 'heard her crying like a baby'.[10] A cast was taken of Ellen's head and hands, forming the basis of a sculpture which is now in the cottage. The funeral cortège, bearing her boat-shaped coffin, journeyed from Smallhythe, where the streets were lined for miles with people and cars, to Golders Green Crematorium in London. Her ashes were placed in a shrine specially created in a room in the cottage, until a year later they were deposited in St Paul's Church, Covent Garden, traditionally 'the actors' church'.

Edy changed a good deal after her mother's death. The changes were noted by Chris who thought 'the resemblance between Edy and her mother became much more apparent';[11] her manner also started to resemble Ellen's curious mixture of authority and charm. She received hundreds of letters from those who had admired and adored Ellen. One said, 'Think of your mother as if she were in the next room to you, only with the door shut.'[12]

At some point, in the midst of her grief, Edy decided to devote her energy and talents – and Chris's, of course – to preserving the memory of Ellen's work and reputation and ensuring her place in history. In dedicating the later years of their lives to honouring a legend, they were also reserving a smaller place in history for themselves. They set to work annotating and revising the Ellen Terry memoirs (which Chris had virtually ghost-written in the first place). Edy also gave Chris the job of editing the voluminous correspondence between Ellen and George Bernard Shaw, which was initially published against the wishes of Ted Craig, who loathed Shaw.

In December 1928, the Ellen Terry Memorial Committee held its inaugural meeting at London's Globe Theatre to set out its aims and objectives. It was decided to turn Smallhythe into a permanent memorial to Terry: the cottage would become a museum, her bedroom would be preserved as it was the day she died and the barn would be converted into a theatre. With her customary panache, Edy threw herself into the project and, give or take a few holes in its thatched roof, the Barn Theatre was ready in time for the first Ellen Terry Memorial Gala in July 1929 and the museum was receiving its first visitors.

For the first two years, the only performances at the theatre were the Terry memorials, financed entirely by Edy. But in 1932, the Memorial Trustees agreed to take over responsibility for Smallhythe's upkeep in return for the option to buy the cottage and theatre. Chris summed up their disappointment, 'We are still honouring Ellen Terry on the cheap'.

That same year, Edy established the subscription-based Barn Theatre Society and four or five shows a year were performed at the barn from 1932 to 1939. Somehow she persuaded the cream of London's theatre to rehearse her shows while performing their own in the West End, trekking down to Smallhythe for a single Sunday performance, and all for expenses only. The Second World War put an end to the shows, but Edy resolutely continued to commemorate her mother's anniversary with readings, symposiums and staged scenes from Shakespeare. One year, the gala was infused with a good deal of unscripted drama: during rehearsals, an adder was rumoured to have been found under the seats and, during the performance, an electrical short-circuit threatened to bring the curtain down on the precarious timber-and-thatch barn. Smallhythe also became known for a different, if equally popular and energetic, Edy production: her jumble sales. At one, Una Troubridge noted Chris's 'shrunken vests' among the heaps of discarded clothes.

During the 1930s, Edy's cousin, Olive Chaplin, set up home in a house opposite her aunt and companions with a woman architect twenty years her junior. Her name was Lucy Gow but she insisted on being known as 'Lucien'. Edy thought that Lucy/Lucien was a good influence on Olive, who was something of a lush and a spendthrift. As 'Lucien' Gow, she also became part of the Smallhythe establishment, credited in the programmes as 'Electrician', which was later elevated to 'lighting under the direction of Lucien Gow'. Anthony Thomas, later director of the Barn Theatre, wryly observed that, given the state of the theatre's lighting equipment, Lucy/Lucien should have gone back to the drawing-board.

The 1930s brought 'The Boys' other new, more important friends, including the women who were then (and, some would claim, still are) the world's most famous lesbian couple: Radclyffe Hall and her partner, Lady Una Troubridge. The pair had set up home in Rye, just a few miles down the road from Smallhythe. They were invited to one of Edy's pageants in July 1930 and Edy and 'The Boys' became regular visitors to the Hall–Troubridge home. In July 1931, they were present for another Barn performance, with John Gielgud and Edith Evans acting scenes from Shakespeare. They even managed to pull off a minor social miracle: to get the trio to leave the house in the evening, for dinner in Rye. They would spend hours gossiping in the shed at Smallhythe that Tony used for a studio. Una Troubridge later reflected that the times spent at Smallhythe were some of their happiest together. Tony made a touching gesture to the deeply religious pair by giving them what was believed to be a relic of the True Cross, supposedly passed on through her family for 150 years. Una always kept this relic in the shrine to St Anthony in her bedroom. When she adapted Colette's *Cheri* for the stage, which opened at the Prince of Wales Theatre on 26 October 1931, Edy and Chris travelled up for the opening night. However, the production was a resounding flop and Hall and Una fled back to Rye. At one point, they made tentative plans to build a house near Smallhythe but it was the usually diplomatic Tony whom they found stomping around the field declaring, 'We can't possibly have a house out here!' The plans were promptly dropped.

Perhaps it was just as well. Una Troubridge was wont to refer to Chris as 'a sort of Ugly Duchess' and dubbed her and Edy 'the Handsome Pair'.[13] And in any case, the stability of the Smallhythe set-up was soon to be badly shaken. Ironically, it would be the 'Ugly Duchess', the 'willing slave', who, against all the odds, was to throw a spanner in the emotional works – a spanner called Vita Sackville-West.

Of course – who else? Vita Sackville-West – one of the few women in history to get everything she ever set her sights on, except one: her ancestral home, Knole, which she lost to her cousin, Eddy Sackville-West, by the mere fact of being a woman. With the sense of place and heritage characteristic of the nobility, it was arguably her greatest loss and one she never forgot or forgave. This may partly account for her selfishness in her relationships with other women.

She first met Chris in July 1932 at the Ellen Terry memorial performance of *Twelfth Night*, featuring John Gielgud and Peggy Ashcroft. As a return favour, Vita invited the Smallhythe trio to Sissinghurst the following month. While Vita was showing her guests around her bedroom, Chris later recalled, 'I felt my whole being dissolve in love. I have never, never ceased to love her from that moment.'[14] She began to keep a journal of her love for Vita.

Vita was invited to read her poem, 'The Land', at the Barn Theatre in September 1932. After a rehearsal, she wrote to a friend, 'The producer [Edy] is the most tearing old Lesbian – but without any charms for me, I hasten to add....'[15] Among those who attended the performance were Virginia Woolf and Stephen Spender, who succumbed to a fit of the giggles during the reading and was reprimanded by an appalled Woolf.

Meanwhile, Vita took Chris on a visit to her former home, Long Barn, gave her a blue necklace from Persia and visited her at the Covent Garden flat. According to Chris, Vita informed her that, although the list of those she really loved was a short one, 'now I was on it'.[16] The idea of Vita as Orlando captured Chris's romantic imagination: 'I could love you in breeches, or in skirts, or in any other garments; or in none.'[17] Finally, one night in late December 1932, they slept together. What the swooning Chris did not realize was that Vita was on the rebound from another broken female love affair and was merely taking consolation in Chris and would soon embark on one of her lengthy journeys abroad.

While Vita was away, Christ wrote many letters to 'My Lord Orlando', but Vita did not exactly hurry back to her side after returning from her travels six months later. When they did meet up, they went for a drive and Vita told her that their first night together had also been their last. Chris was hurt but never stopped loving her.

Despite all her previous claims to be free of jealousy, Edy was enraged by Chris's infatuation with and love for Vita, and there were some furious rows before it became clear that her feelings were not being reciprocated. Virginia Woolf referred to poor Chris as Vita's 'mule-faced harridan'. She also immortalized Edy in her last novel *Between The Acts*, as the energetic producer, Miss La Trobe, who organizes a pageant in the grounds of Pointz Hall, a country manor house, just before the outbreak of the Second World War. Miss La Trobe is portrayed as an outsider in the village; mistrusted and constantly falling out with her 'cast', she strides about in a smock frock, often with a whip in one hand. The locals call her 'Bossy' behind her back.

Eventually, Vita began to make excuses for not seeing Chris, who complained about this to their mutual friend, Ethel Smyth. She refused to see Chris alone but invited the Smallhythe trio to Sissinghurst. Chris got revenge – of a sort – when Vita's book, *Saint Joan of Arc*, came out in 1936 and the spurned St John lambasted the work in her journal and, more damagingly, in the review pages of the *New Statesman*.

In 1939, a dinner was held in Edy's honour at the Savoy in recognition of her services to theatre, presided over by Dame Sybil Thorndike. A message of congratulations from Queen Mary was read out, and Vita Sackville-West was among those who gave speeches. Edy was presented with a scroll inscribed with all the names of those at the dinner plus a cheque.

Throughout the war, 'The Boys' stayed at Smallhythe while bombs rained down on the Kent and Sussex countryside. In July 1946, aged seventy-seven, Edy produced her last show, the Chilham Pageant, despite suffering from rheumatism, arthritis and heart trouble. A fund-raiser for the National Association of Boys' Clubs and the Soldiers', Sailors' and Airmen's Families Association, the pageant was staged at Chilham Castle, a few miles from Canterbury. It told the history of Kent and involved people from ten different towns and villages, including Smallhythe's neighbour, Tenterden.

In March 1947, against doctor's orders, Edy attended the memorial service at St Paul's, Covent Garden, for Ellen Terry's centenary. On 27 March, she and Chris were discussing the next Shakespeare production for the Barn Theatre when she suddenly cried out, 'It's all dark. Who put out the light?', and died. 'The Boys' had lost their 'Master'.

Edy bequeathed the whole of Smallhythe to the National Trust, on condition that Chris and Tony were to be allowed to live in the Priest's House for the rest of their lives. Olive Chaplin was to be the museum's curator. When she died, Edy left little cash, and Chris and Tony had scant means of their own. Vita Sackville-West gave them enough to tide them over until they finalized the agreement with the National Trust. Vita also took pity on Chris who, after losing her partner of forty-eight years, was understandably distraught. She was invited to Sissinghurst for a short stay.

After Edy's death, Chris and Tony continued to take an interest in the shows at the Barn Theatre, occasionally helping out with seat allocations and looking after guests. But increasingly they kept themselves shut away in the Priest's House, seeing no one and being seen by no one. Henry Irving's grandson, Laurence, who was writing his grandfather's biography, tried to talk to them. The door opened a few inches but he got no further than 'Good morning, my name is Laurence Irving' when it was slammed in his face.

The actor Donald Sinden had become friends with Olive Chaplin during the 1950s and took a keen interest in the Terrys and, latterly, Chris and Tony. However, Olive warned him off trying to get past the permanently chained door to meet them. In 1961, Tony, by now in her nineties, was admitted into a nursing home. Not long afterwards, Chris was taken into Tenterden Hospital. The intrepid Sinden tracked her down and was told by nursing staff that 'Miss St John' was 'quite impossible', given to throwing her lunch tray at them. By now, Chris's much-ridiculed thick features had become emaciated and blotchy. Sinden spent several hours with her, talking about Ellen Terry. She asked him to visit her again but he never got the chance. She died in October 1961, in her late eighties, followed within weeks by Tony. They were buried side by side in the tiny graveyard at Smallhythe.

Olive Chaplin cleared out the Priest's House, which was in a filthy state. In the garden shed, which was crammed top to bottom with old copies of *The Times*, she found a tin box containing all of Ellen Terry's letters to her last two husbands. Chaplin decided that Terry would have wanted them destroyed and promptly did so. The rest of the contents of the cottage were sold; Donald Sinden bought many of the items. She later told him that she had been having a rifle through her own boxes of mementoes when she came across a tin container full of dust. Only then did she remember her promise to Edy: to bury her ashes with Chris and Tony. She had been waiting so long – fourteen years – to carry out her cousin's last request that, when the time came, she had forgotten. She promised to 'nip across one day and scatter them on the grave'. We can only assume this happened and that 'The Boys', eventually, were all together again.

There was yet another surprise in store: Violet Pym, the mutual friend who had originally introduced Chris to Vita Sackville-West, went through Chris's papers and discovered the journal she had kept of their affair. Incredibly, she handed it over to Vita. In her study in the tower at Sissinghurst she read the 'horrifying document'.[18] Today, Vita's study contains virtually everything that was in it the day she died; among the items preserved are a number of framed poems and prayers decorated with calligraphy by Chris.

Some of Edy's friends say that it was her bossiness and fastidiousness, her seemingly unquenchable thirst for perfection that alienated her from the London theatrical establishment. Her creativity and energy were remarkable, even if her ideas were occasionally a little over-ambitious; Chris and Tony were fond of remarking, 'Edy has bitten off more than we can chew.' Many were of the opinion that she never received the credit due to her as an important figure in the theatre. Her obituary in *The Times* summed it up well: 'Her devotion to her mother shone out more brightly than the remarkable theatrical talent which never perhaps received its due attention.' She certainly deserved more credit and a better fate, instead of ending up as so many children of the famous do: a pile of forgotten dust.

A few hundred yards from where 'The Boys' are buried, the Ellen Terry Museum at Smallhythe Place remains open to the public, run by the National Trust and elegantly preserved. It houses a remarkable collection of items, chronicling the life and work of Ellen Terry and, in particular, her long partnership with Henry Irving. The Lyceum and Costume Rooms contain many of the costumes and props from their most successful productions together, including the rather gruesome dress she wore as Lady

Macbeth which was decorated entirely with beetle wings. The walls are groaning with photographs and paintings, particularly in the Terry Room – many of them by Tony Atwood, including some of 'The Boys' in Smallhythe's garden. In Ellen's bedroom is the school desk used by Edy and Ted when they were children, and later used by Ellen herself as a writing desk. But perhaps the most symbolic item is to be found in a glass case in the Terry Room: Ellen's 'friendship necklace', made from different-coloured gemstones, each representing a special person in her life. The two largest stones – both round, one green, one orange – were reserved for Edy and Chris.

Notes

1. Ellen Terry, *The Story of My Life* (London, Frederick Muller, 1933), p. 71.
2. Eleanor Adlard (ed.), *Edy: Recollections of Edith Craig* (London, Frederick Muller, 1949), p. 19.
3. Christopher St John, *Hungerheart* (London, Methuen, 1915), p. 57.
4. Joy Melville, *Ellen and Edy* (London, Pandora, 1987), p. 214.
5. *Ibid.*, p. 228.
6. Adlard, *Edy*, p. 123.
7. *Ibid.*, p. 91.
8. Melville, *Ellen and Edy*, p. 231.
9. Adlard, *Edy*, p. 25.
10. Terry, *My Life*, p. 378.
11. Adlard, *Edy*, p. 31.
12. Terry, *My Life*, p. 342.
13. Michael Baker, *Our Three Selves* (London, Hamish Hamilton, 1985), p. 264.
14. Victoria Glendenning, *Vita* (London, Weidenfeld & Nicolson, 1983), p. 250.
15. *Ibid.*
16. *Ibid.*, p. 253.
17. *Ibid.*
18. *Ibid.*, p. 398.

Rosa Bonheur

WHEN you consider Edy Craig's life, it is patently obvious that there were very few people who won her respect or admiration. The standards she set for others were as high as those she set for herself, and few, apart from her mother and her two life partners, could ever hope to live up to them. But there was one notable exception: the woman whom she chose to portray whenever she staged one of her historical feminist pageants – Rosa Bonheur. Why? What was it about this French painter, out of all the remarkable women in Edy's lifetime, that made her the heroine for someone with such exacting standards?

In an area of the arts where women often fell by the wayside while their male counterparts prospered, Bonheur scaled heights of commercial and critical success previously unknown to a female artist. Furthermore, she achieved her success while living openly and uncompromisingly with other women, largely independent of her parents. All this would inevitably strike a chord with someone like Edy Craig, bound inextricably to her mother's fame and achievements, and who may have found that the London theatrical establishment was not as accepting of overt lesbians as it was of overt gay men.

Rosa was born Marie-Rosalie Bonheur in Bordeaux on 16 March 1822. Her father, Raimond, was an artist, her mother, Sophie, the well-educated daughter of a Bordeaux merchant. Raimond was a member of the Saint-Simonian movement, whose radical politics advocated a utopian world of economic socialism and sexual equality. It was Sophie who encouraged her daughter to draw and soon the young Rosa was spending hours sketching the farm animals on the country estates of her mother's friends and relatives.

Despite Sophie's background and connections, the Bonheurs were poor: Raimond found it difficult to support his growing family by selling his own paintings and teaching (by 1828, another daughter and two sons had been born). Sophie, a skilled pianist, supplemented their meagre income by giving piano lessons to local children. When Rosa was six years old, Raimond decided that the family would fare better in Paris. They set up home in the Rue St Antoine, in rooms over a public baths. Opposite was a pork butcher's shop which had, as its shop-sign, the carved figure of a boar; Rosa was often to be found stroking this figure. She later recalled, 'This was, perhaps, one of my earliest manifestations of a love for the dumb world.'[1]

But while Raimond was successful in finding new friends who shared his political beliefs, he was less successful in fulfilling his artistic ambitions. At one point, he even went to live in a Saint-Simonian 'monastery', where his family were only allowed to visit him on Sundays. And, for all the Saint-Simonians' belief in sexual equality, it was Sophie Bonheur who bore the brunt of their poverty while Raimond was finding outlets for his idealism. She would trudge miles looking for the cheapest vegetables and, as well as giving piano lessons, she did piecework at night, sewing garters. In later years, Rosa spoke with some bitterness of her exhausted mother's travails. Rosa herself did not adapt easily to big city life: even the bread tasted different, she later recalled. At school, she played with the boys and was involved in her fair share of fistfights.

Four years after the move to Paris, Sophie Bonheur died. Rosa later recalled, 'My mother died from exhaustion after nursing me during my illness with scarlet fever. Her remains were buried in a potter's field.'[2] Rosa was eleven.

Initially, Raimond wanted his daughter to become a dressmaker's apprentice but eventually he sent her to his friends, the Bissons, who ran a decorative painting and engraving business, which was much more to Rosa's liking. However, Raimond decided she still needed a proper education and, mistakenly, sent her to boarding school. Before long, she was expelled for leading a 'cavalry charge' across the head's prize rose-bed. Little wonder that, in 1829, her mother had written, 'I don't know what Rosalie will be, but I have a conviction that she will be no ordinary woman.'[3]

Raimond gave in to the inevitable and Rosa's education was conducted at home. Until she was fourteen, she spent each day in her father's studio where he would give her different tasks to do: sometimes it would be a still-life drawing, other times it might be an engraving. Her first painting was of a bunch of cherries. Eventually, Rosa enrolled at the Louvre to study painting and sculpture, one of the youngest students to be admitted. There, she began to copy the works of Dutch *animaliers*.

At the age of sixteen she started going to slaughterhouses to study the anatomy of animals at close hand. 'One must know what is under their skin,' she explained, 'otherwise your animal will look like a mat rather than a tiger.'[4]

As well as the influence of the Saint-Simonians, Rosa's own beliefs were heavily influenced by the Abbé Felicité de Lammenais, a radical Catholic theologist and philosopher, and an advocate of universal suffrage. In particular, she was obviously influenced by Lammenais' views on art and nature: 'Art is not a simple imitation of nature; it must reveal ... the intense principle, the ideal beauty that only the spirit perceives. ...'[5]

Gradually, the Bonheur apartment started to fill up with animals, including a pet sheep and myriad birds. Eventually, when Rosa was nineteen, Raimond moved his family to slightly larger accommodation, which was promptly filled up with chickens, ducks, quails, finches, rabbits and a goat.

In 1842, her father remarried, to Marguerite Peyrol, a young widow. Although all the young Bonheurs liked their new step-mother, it was a particularly welcome development for Rosa, who was now freed from the responsibilities foisted on her as the eldest daughter in a motherless family. And by then, she had renewed her relationship with the young woman whose lifelong love and devotion to Rosa and her work played such an integral part in her success.

Rosa Bonheur and Nathalie Micas had known each other as young children; Madame Micas sold animal skins to Madame

Bonheur, for making (among other things) shuttlecocks. Rosa would make fun of Nathalie's pale complexion and sickly demeanour. Indeed, Nathalie's parents were so convinced that their daughter would not reach maturity that Monsieur Micas commissioned Rosa's father to paint her portrait when she was twelve. Instead of mocking her frail friend, Rosa adopted a more protective attitude towards her. From then on, she became a frequent and welcome visitor to the Micas household.

Rosa first exhibited at the annual Paris Salon in 1841. Although the two paintings submitted were not singled out for any praise by the Salon's judges or critics, it was still a considerable achievement for a woman a mere nineteen years old. The following year, she submitted three paintings and a sculpture; this caught the attention of one critic, who compared it to the work of Antoine Barye, the major animal sculptor of the time. Within three years of her first appearance at the Salon, Rosa's paintings began to sell and she used the money to travel throughout France, studying different breeds of farm animals. When she exhibited at the Salon of 1845, her work was awarded a third-class medal and critical acclaim was heaped upon her. Three years later, she received a gold medal.

Her success meant that she could rent a studio for the first time, and she set to work on a major canvas, *Ploughing in the Nivernais*, commissioned by the government for exhibition at the Salon. Rosa intended to 'celebrate with my brush the art of tracing the furrows from which comes the bread that nourishes all humanity'.[6] Shortly before the 1849 Salon, Raimond Bonheur died; although Rosa grieved, her ambivalent feelings towards her father and the way he had treated her mother remained unresolved. But there was little time for grieving or looking back: Rosa and her sister, Juliette, were asked to replace Raimond as head of the government's School of Drawing for Young Girls. Shortly after this appointment, *Ploughing in the Nivernais* was shown at the Salon; it won universal acclaim from critics and audiences alike: the *Gazette des Beaux Arts* praised 'the intense love that it evidenced for the beings and the things pertaining to that nature'.[7] The picture was subsequently bought by the Musée du Luxembourg for 3,000 francs. To complete her triumph, two brothers, the Tedescos, became her dealers. From now on, there would be no more false starts: for the rest of her life, Rosa Bonheur would know nothing but success.

Soon after her father's death, she moved in with Nathalie and the Micas. While some of Rosa's family disapproved of her match with Nathalie, the Micas family seemed to have no problem in accepting the partnership, to such an extent that, in 1848, Monsieur Micas summoned the two women to his deathbed to give them his blessing and to encourage them to stay together.

Rosa often spoke of her relationship with an ambiguous mixture of reserve and openness. In a letter to one friend she declared, 'My private life is nobody's concern. I have only to thank God for the protection he has always granted me by giving me a guardian angel in my friend.'[8] Rosa's god-daughter, Rosa Mathieu, observed, 'Nathalie Micas literally worshipped Rosa Bonheur'[9] – a view held by many who knew them. Rosa said of Nathalie, 'She was my equal in everything and my superior in many things.'[10] One of Rosa's closest friends wrote of their relationship, 'Nathalie made herself small, ungrudgingly, so that Rosa might become greater.'[11]

One of the myths surrounding Nathalie's contribution to Rosa's work was that she was able to 'hypnotize' animals so they would keep still while Rosa painted them – something Rosa always denied. She was always inventing things, including the Micas express train-brake. She and Rosa built a special area in the gardens so the brake could be tested, where it was found to work perfectly. But no one would accept the design, because it had been made by a woman. A few years later, an Englishman took the design, made some minor changes and sold it to the British railroads. She also claimed to have veterinary skills, which she was always keen to demonstrate on any member of the menagerie who fell ill. Nathalie also painted, but the pictures tended to be rather twee: messily daubed kittens playing with balls of wool and the like. But while others would laugh at her behind her back, Rosa – the supreme animal painter – was always full of encouragement.

Nathalie was indeed something of a figure of fun with many who knew her: she claimed to be of Spanish descent and always dressed in red and black. She also was given to wearing a ridiculously ostentatious plumed hat which always provoked howls of laughter. Even Rosa was given to say about her partner, 'Sometimes

I think Nathalie would have made a fine wife for one of the court jesters of the olden time.'[12]

In 1851, after a lengthy holiday with Nathalie in the Pyrenees, Rosa started visiting the horse market at Boulevard de l'Hôpital, where she made a series of preparatory studies for the painting which was to launch her on to the international art scene. Something else at this time would also bring her another sort of fame, even notoriety – her appearance.

Rosa always said she wore men's clothes out of necessity and for practical purposes only, rather than out of a desire to shock, *à la* George Sand. At home, or in the studio, she usually wore loose trousers and long smocks. When she started to visit slaughterhouses and animal markets, she made no concession to conventional women's clothes; she always maintained that her appearance enabled her to frequent the places she needed to visit for her research. Even so, some of the workers in these all-male domains would still, as Rosa described it, 'make themselves as disagreeable to me as they possibly could'.[13] However, by the time she started frequenting the horse markets, she had perfected her cross-dressing to such an extent that she was able to wander among the horses and their handlers without hindrance. Eventually, she was issued with police certificates – *permission de travestissement* – renewable every six months, which allowed her to wear male clothes in public places, except for 'spectacles, balls or other public meeting places'. Curiously, the permits were given 'for reasons of health' and were countersigned by her doctor.

In one episode straight out of *Victor/Victoria*, Rosa was arrested in the street by a policeman who thought she was a man dressed as a woman. When he tried to march her off, she hit him so hard he was even more convinced that he was arresting a man. When Rosa was brought before the police magistrate, the hapless officer received a dressing-down and the dressed-up artist received profuse apologies.

Despite the butch attire, she was not the swarthy figure many imagined her to be. She was of medium height, with delicate hands and feet she was proud of. However, she could only be persuaded out of her male drag for formal occasions, when she would make a minor compromise by wearing a black skirt with a waistcoat buttoned to the top. Unfortunately, she had a penchant for wearing rather large, ill-fitting hats and she was mortified one day when, strolling through a Paris street, she heard a parrot call out 'Ha, ha – that hat!'[14]

It is not so easy to reclaim Rosa as a feminist icon. In terms of the sexes, she found neither entirely to her liking. She certainly never forgave the male of the species for what had happened to her mother and believed that, once married, women were condemned to live the life of a 'subaltern'. She once told a man who, on seeing her out riding with a male friend, had remarked that her companion's wife should be worried, 'Oh dear sir, if you only knew how little I care for your sex, you wouldn't get such queer ideas into your head. The fact is, in the way of males, I like only the bulls I paint.'[15] When she argued with her dealers, she would berate them, 'Go home to your mother and mend stockings or make petit point.'[16]

But she also appeared to have little time for most women. She told her students at the School of Drawing, 'I have no patience with women who ask permission to think. Let women establish their claims by great and good works, and not by conventions.'[17] In a letter to her brother, Isidore, she said of their sister, Juliette, 'She has too much of the motherly instinct in her for my taste, and I am afraid she will get more happiness out of having children than from an artistic career.'[18] It is probably true to say that her relationships with animals were more intense and spiritually fulfilling than with most of the humans she knew.

The Horse Fair was unveiled at the 1853 Salon where it received not only critical and public praise but the Royal seal of approval from the Emperor and Empress. Thousands of lithographic reproductions of the painting were sold in France and England. Eventually it was bought by a leading European art dealer, Ernest Gambart, for the incredible sum of 40,000 francs. To celebrate, Rosa whisked Nathalie off for another holiday in Spain. On their return, Rosa and the Micas moved to a new home with a purpose-built studio, big enough, finally, for *all* its residents – human or otherwise. The household ran like clockwork: Rosa worked in her studio, while Nathalie and her mother took care of the domestic responsibilities. Rosa reported to a friend, 'Our artist household is getting on very well. My wife has much talent and the children don't prevent us from painting pictures.'[19] Her 'artist household', of course, included not only Micas *mere* and Micas *fille* but horses, goats, sheep, dogs, lapwings, hoopoes, monkeys, donkeys and an occasional otter.

In 1856, Rosa and Nathalie left for a tour of England and Scotland, organized by Gambart. They were presented to Queen Victoria, and met a number of British artists including Millais, John Ruskin and, most notably, Sir Edwin Landseer, England's own master animal painter. His engraving of *The Horse Fair* was dedicated to the Queen. When Landseer, always quaintly described as 'a confirmed bachelor', jokingly offered to become 'Sir Edwin Bonheur', the London art world was soon rippling with the rumour that the two greatest living animal painters were to be married. Apart from this slight glitch, the tour was wildly successful: wherever she went Rosa was fêted, feasted and toasted. She filled dozens of notebooks and sketchbooks, particularly in Scotland, where she paid careful attention to the unusual Highland oxen, cattle and sheep.

In 1857 *The Horse Fair* was sold to an American dealer and went on a two-year tour of major American cities. America went wild for it: the *United States Journal* offered a free print of the work to every new subscriber, who would then be the owner of 'a magnificent specimen of art ... unsurpassed in interest by anything ever before issued on this side of the Atlantic'.[20] It was headlined, 'The World's Greatest Animal Picture' – a little off the mark but then, in a country where a horse was worth as much as a man's life, Rosa's fine study was always going to be popular.

In 1860 Rosa and Nathalie bought the Chateau de By, a manor house near the Forest of Fontainebleau, with acres of sprawling woodland and pasture. Naturally, mother – and the menagerie – went too. With the acquisition of this vast new home, more exotic animals soon began to appear: gazelles, deer, elk, Icelandic ponies, even a yak – and, eventually, her beloved lions, including her favourite, Fathma. When she moved to By, Rosa stepped down as co-director of the School of Drawing.

Life at the new chateau ran as smoothly as it had done in Paris, under the expert supervision of Nathalie and her mother, and

Rosa settled down to enjoying her fame and fortune and fulfilling her commissions. She spent much of her time with her ever-increasing menagerie or shut away in her large studio, working on canvasses and smoking endless roll-ups. Nonetheless, there were plenty of visitors – some more welcome than others – to interrupt her.

One day in 1864, the Empress Eugénie paid the household an unannounced visit; Rosa was working in her paint-spattered smock and Nathalie was taking a bath in the small tub by the studio. When the Empress was announced, Rosa shut the bathroom door and went to meet her Royal visitor, who was there to present her with the Grand Cross of the Legion of Honour, the first woman ever to receive this award. The Empress said she 'had wished that the last act of my regency be dedicated to showing that in my eyes genius has no sex'.[21] Nathalie, shut away in the bathroom, was furious at missing such an important moment. The composer, Georges Bizet, wrote a song to commemorate the award, with lyrics by Auguste Cain, the animal sculptor:

> *Our Rosa was never coquettish,*
> *Interested herself not with flowers or ribbons.*
> *The Empress wanted her dress*
> *To have one, and of the most magnificent kind.*

It was not the only honour bestowed upon Rosa in her lifetime; other awards included: Honorary Member of the Pennsylvania Academy of Fine Arts; Honorary Member of the Société des Artistes Belges; The Cross of San Carlos of Mexico from Emperor Maximilian and Empress Carlotta; a Member of the Académie des Beaux-Arts of Antwerp; Spain's Commander's Cross of the Royal Order of Isabella and the Mérit des Beaux-Arts de Saxe-Coburg-Gotha.

In 1865, she made history again when a quarter-size version of *The Horse Fair*, painted ten years before, went on show at the National Gallery in London – the first painting by a living artist to be exhibited there.

The tranquillity of life at By was interrupted by the Franco-Prussian War, which began in 1870. Rosa was all for taking up arms and attempting to stop the Prussian army crossing the Seine, but her neighbours in the village were not convinced. When the invaders did arrive, there was no bloodshed; but Rosa refused to kowtow to the Prussian officers encamped at her home.

Once peace had returned to France, Rosa's interest turned from farm animals to zoo animals, in particular lions, tigers and panthers. Soon, the commissions for paintings of her newest subjects were flowing in. In 1875, Rosa began renting a villa in Nice from her agent, Gambart; she decided to spend winters there because of Nathalie's precarious state of health. It was never likely that Nathalie Micas would outlive her partner and she died on 22 June 1889, aged sixty-five. Rosa had lost the woman 'whom I had loved more and more as we advanced in life'.[22] After Nathalie's death, Rosa began to lose interest in her work and life. 'She alone knew me and I, her only friend, knew what she was worth,'[23] she said. 'Her loss broke my heart and it was a long time before I found any relief in my work from this bitter ache.'[24] But, within months, several things happened which went some way to restoring her zest for life.

Colonel William 'Buffalo Bill' Cody was touring France with his Wild West Show that year and decided to pay Rosa a visit. The Colonel presented her with a collection of Sioux buckskin clothes and a set of Osage bow and arrows. His show caused a sensation in Paris and so it was almost logical that France's most celebrated animal painter should commit America's best-known cowboy to canvas. The story goes that, years later, Cody, while away on tour, was told his home in Nebraska was on fire and replied, 'Save the Rosa Bonheur and let the flames take the rest.'[25] As well as painting Cody's portrait (which still remains her best-known picture in America, after *The Horse Fair*), Rosa also visited the native Americans who travelled with the show. She spent weeks at their camp near the Bois du Boulogne, sketching them, their buffaloes and their horses for a series of extraordinary paintings. Her experience with Cody and his roadshow gave her more pleasure than anything else for years, and the sketches she made kept her working on Wild West paintings for the rest of her life.

Another visitor that year was John Arbuckle, a wealthy coffee merchant from New York and President of the Royal Horse

Association. Arbuckle had sent Rosa some wild mustangs a few years earlier and wanted to see them. Accompanying him was a young American painter, Anna Klumpke, who was working as his interpreter. Anna had been born in San Francisco but her mother moved the family to Paris. Among the toys given to young Anna in America were a print of *The Horse Fair* and a doll dressed in Bonheur drag. Before the family left America, Anna suffered severe injuries in an accident, which left her lame. Once in Paris, she was trained at the Académie Julian and embarked on a successful career as a portrait painter, receiving commissions from both sides of the Atlantic.

In 1894, Rosa received her last, and most historic, award: Officier de la Légion d'Honneur – the first woman ever to receive this honour. Soon after, Anna Klumpke visited her again. When she returned, three years later, to paint Rosa's portrait, she was asked to stay. The Klumpkes were not happy about the situation, despite Rosa's assurances. She wrote to Anna's mother, explaining that they had decided to 'associate our lives'[26] – an ambiguous term if ever there was one. To her new partner she declared, 'This will be a divine marriage of two souls.'[27] Mrs Klumpke replied that she was glad her daughter would be 'considered as a little sister' – either she was being wilfully ignorant or the message had lost something in translation. Whatever people thought, within months, Rosa began dictating notes to Anna for use in a future biography and also drew up a new will, bequeathing everything to her new 'associate'.

Unfortunately, in her later years, there was a less pleasant, more insidious development: anti-Semitism. In the late nineteenth century, France was suffering a particularly virulent bout of this unfathomable affliction. Rosa had always been the focus of malicious gossip, partly because of her success, partly because of her appearance and lifestyle. But, almost from nowhere, the rumour spread that she was Jewish: in some circles she became known as 'that Jewess' – it was not meant as a compliment. The rumour alleged that her real name was 'Rosa Mazel-Tov', the Hebrew translation of 'Bonheur' and that her father had regularly attended a synagogue. Rosa was greatly distressed by the rising tide of anti-Semitism, not so much for the rumours concerning her, but because she believed it threatened the democracy of France.

In May 1899, Rosa made a visit to Paris; the weather was unusually cold and she returned to By with flu. It quickly turned into pneumonia and she sank rapidly. She died on 25 May. Her funeral service was held in the church at By on 29 May, followed by a second service in Père Lachaise cemetery in Paris. She was buried with Nathalie and the other members of the Micas family.

Within a relatively short time after her death, Rosa's reputation seemed to plummet. For example, in 1888, one of her paintings fetched £4,200 at auction; in 1929, the same painting went for £46. Some art historians have blamed this dramatic slump on original over-estimates and valuations of her work. However, when the contents of her studio were auctioned the year after her death, there were still plenty of keen buyers for the 1,835 works on offer.

Some critics decried her work, denouncing it as too laboured, devoid of any personality; that her precision over-egged the pudding. Her paintings, which had been created from a combination of correct technique and anatomical knowledge, were described in her obituary in the *New York Tribune* as lacking 'the spark of genius which places a picture apart', and their creator as practising 'a kind of dignified realism'.[28] Nonetheless, during and after her lifetime, she remained a touchstone for other women painters who often found themselves compared to her: the Dutch artist Marie Collaert was dubbed 'the Flemish Rosa Bonheur', while Elizabeth Thompson Butler, famous for her paintings of battle scenes, was called 'the English Rosa Bonheur' – the only possible reason being that her pictures of battlefields included some horses. One artist, Louise Abbema, recalled, 'While still a little girl, I heard Rosa Bonheur much spoken of, and it was her talent and her fame that decided me to become an artist.'[29]

Meanwhile, as art critics chewed over the bones of Rosa's reputation, her 'heir', Anna Klumpke, set about fulfilling one of her last requests: to write the 'official' Bonheur biography – Rosa had always said that 'no man could write my biography'.[30] She had also stipulated that Anna be buried with her and Nathalie – a wish that was fulfilled in 1945. In death, as in life, Rosa's devoted partners stayed with her. Their joint grave in Père Lachaise bears the inscription 'L'amitié, c'est l'affection divine' – 'Friendship is divine affection.'

Notes

1. Theodore Stanton (ed.), *Reminiscences of Rosa Bonheur* (London, Andrew Melrose, 1910), p. 6.
2. Dore Ashton and Denise Browne Hare, *Rosa Bonheur: A Life and A Legend* (London, Secker and Warburg, 1981), p. 26.
3. Stanton, *Reminiscences*, p. 13.
4. Ashton and Browne Hare, *Life and Legend*, p. 41.
5. *Ibid.*, p. 38.
6. *Ibid.*, p 69.
7. *Ibid.*, p. 70.
8. Stanton, *Reminiscences*, p. 102.
9. *Ibid.*, p. 99.
10. *Ibid.*, p. 102.
11. *Ibid.*, pp. 97–8.
12. *Ibid.*, p. 89.
13. Ashton and Browne Hare, *Life and Legend*, p. 52.
14. Stanton, *Reminiscences*, p. 39.
15. Ashton and Browne Hare, *Life and Legend*, p. 59.
16. *Ibid.*, p. 100.
17. *Ibid.*
18. *Ibid.*, p. 101.
19. Stanton, *Reminiscences*, p. 269.
20. Ashton and Browne Hare, *Life and Legend*, p. 87.
21. Stanton, *Reminiscences*, p. 13.
22. *Ibid.*, p. 102.
23. *Ibid.*, pp. 97–8.
24. Ashton and Browne Hare, *Life and Legend*, p. 120.
25. *Ibid.*, p. 155.
26. *Ibid.*, p. 180.
27. *Ibid.*
28. *Ibid.*, p. 185.
29. Stanton, *Reminiscences*, p. 140.
30. Anna Elizabeth Klumpke, *Memoirs of an Artist* (Paris, 1908), p. 107.

Selma Lagerlöf

TONI Morrison was awarded the Nobel Prize for Literature in 1993 and, as is customary (and correct), commentators were keen to point out how few women had ever won it. Newspaper reports on Morrison's success were usually accompanied by the full list of previous female winners: some, like the South African novelist, Nadine Gordimer, were familiar names. But the first name on the list was always greeted (by British readers, anyway) with the response: '*Who?*' The subject of this oft-repeated query was, in fact, one of the most popular and widely translated European writers of her time, honoured and revered in her own country on the level of royalty. Eleven films were made from her books, of which the best-known was instrumental in launching the international career of Greta Garbo. Her children's books are still favourites throughout the world. And, of course, she was the first woman writer to win literature's most coveted prize. However, it is highly likely that the only person least surprised or upset by her relative anonymity today would have been the writer herself. For Selma Lagerlöf, the unassuming country girl who toiled quietly and diligently to the top of her profession, never ceased to be slightly bemused by her popularity and accepted the success, honours and public affection bestowed on her with an unaffected modesty that many contemporary writers could learn from.

By the end of her long life, Lagerlöf had virtually become a legend in her own lifetime – another irony that was surely not lost on her, as legends, myths and traditional folk-tales were the anvil upon which she forged and shaped her raw talent as a storyteller.

Selma Ottiliana Lovisa Lagerlöf was born on 20 November 1858, at Mårbacka, in the central rural region of Värmland, the fourth child in a family of two boys and three girls. Her mother, Lovisa, was the daughter of a wealthy merchant and mine-owner. Her father, Erik Lagerlöf, was a Lieutenant in the Värmland Regiment. His father had been the Regimental Paymaster, a post which Erik expected to inherit. Instead, he took over the family estate at Mårbacka and settled down to become an enthusiastic, if impractical, gentleman farmer and country squire. The Lagerlöfs had been resident in the district since the seventeenth century. Selma's ancestors included Petrus Lagerlöf, the State Historian in the seventeenth century, and the church in Jösse-Ny contained many paintings of past Lagerlöfs.

Then, as now, most of Sweden's population lived in its few large cities and towns. In the nineteenth century, over a third of the country's six million people lived in the urban centres; the rest dwelt in isolated farms and sparse villages, where the winters were long and hard, the summers short and sweet. Värmland was a region of thick forests, inhabited by wolves and bears. The River Klar ran through it and there were also numerous lakes. The district was rich in mineral ores and the wealth generated by mining engendered the rise of affluent families in the eighteenth and nineteenth centuries. They lived on large estates where, as well as stock farming, they ran charcoal-burning plants and sawmills. Apart from Selma Lagerlöf, other Värmland notables included the satirist Anna Maria Lenngren, Erick Gustav Geijer, the philosopher and historian, and the sculptor Johan Nicklas Byström.

The family house itself was sparsely furnished, with faded wallpaper and threadbare rugs covering the floors. Erik Lagerlöf was more adept at the social niceties of farm life than day-to-day practicalities, but Selma adored him, particularly his zest for life.

Mårbacka hosted parties in abundance and Erik turned his birthday party into the district festival, with pageants, music and fireworks. With opera, theatre and concerts many miles away, country communities made their own entertainment. Moreover, no one was left out: the district's down-and-outs, many of whom were ex-soldiers, were embraced by the estate-owners, invited into their homes and fed. These old warriors would pay their way by recounting tall tales of past battles and bottles – meat and drink to a young child's imagination. And, for Selma Lagerlöf, they were welcome additions to the stories of local legends told to her by her grandparents, parents and servants at Mårbacka. As well as these stories, there were also the myths that surrounded current events of the day to fuel the fires of her imagination. The best example of this concerned the death of the popular Prince Gustav in 1873: a rumour spread that he was, in fact, alive and well and living in Norway with a commoner wife. His grieving subjects would rather believe their beloved Prince was a disgraced exile than that he was simply dead. After all, real heroes could not die.

Selma spent most of her childhood in poor health. Admittedly, after the birth of her younger sister, Gerda, it was thought she sometimes feigned illness to get attention. However, one ailment was certainly genuine enough. In the summer of 1862, the family went for a bathe in the spring at Ås. Soon afterwards, Selma developed paralysis in her legs (her mother and uncle had suffered a similar affliction as children). She showed little improvement until a year later, when the family took a holiday in the small seaside resort, Strömstad. Although Selma recovered most of her mobility, one hip remained stiff. This left her with a limp which she disguised by always walking slowly. Years later, when her close friend Valborg Olander expressed some envy of Selma's success, she replied, 'How would you like to have an infirmity that is constantly on your mind?' But she remained philosophical about it: 'It is this disability that has forced me to sit still, to look within myself and that is the reason why I became a writer.'[1]

When she was nine, her father sent her to Stockholm to stay with her uncle while she received specialist treatment for her hip. During this stay, she was introduced to the novels of Walter Scott and saw her first opera and theatre. Her early reading also included the works of Hans Christian Andersen and the *Arabian Nights*.

In 1864, her beloved grandmother – her first storyteller – died, an early loss which devastated Selma. The stories her grandmother had told her were to be the foundation of her literary career – and more. 'It was as if the door to a wonderful magic world had been locked and there was no one now who knew how to open it,'[2] she later recalled. Her Aunt Ottiliana – known as 'Aunt Nana' – helped to fill the void and she became as important a figure in Selma's childhood as her parents, spending every summer at Mårbacka.

Selma and Gerda were educated at home by a series of governesses. In the evenings, there would be storytelling and readings. Selma had also begun to write. Initially, she tried her hand at writing plays, inspired by the grandiose performances she had seen at the Stockholm theatres. She began to write poetry, none of which has survived. At a wedding in 1880, Selma was one of the bridesmaids. In reply to the traditional bridesmaids' toast, she read one of her poems. Among the wedding guests was Eva Fryxell, a writer and notable figure in Stockholm's literary and political circles. She asked Selma to send her some more of her poems and promised to try and find her a publisher, but she was unsuccessful and Selma's work was returned to her some months later. Undeterred, she decided to leave Värmland to complete her education. In 1881, she went to Sjöberg's Lyceum in Stockholm and then took the entrance exam for the Women Teachers' College, where she spent the next three years.

It was not until she was settled in Stockholm that she recognized what an abundant wealth of raw source material her childhood and homeland had put at her disposal. Gradually, the threads of a collection of linked stories were interwoven: the drunken ex-soldiers who dined at the Lagerlöf table and entertained with their exaggerated tales of heroism and romanticism; the age-old myths passed on to her by her grandmother and Aunt Nana; and the Värmland landscape, which shaped and influenced its people spiritually and emotionally. Initially, she struggled to find an acceptable literary form which could contain it all, and for the next ten years she patiently and painstakingly worked on the epic *Gösta Berling's Saga*, the adventures of a drunken ex-preacher, poet and 'heroic scamp'.

She was popular with her fellow students but her closest companion during her college days was one Gurli Linder. It was Linder who, in 1886, passed on a selection of Selma's poems to Baroness Sophie Adlersparre, pioneer of the Swedish women's movement and publisher of the newspaper *Dagny*. Adlersparre wrote to Selma, praising her sonnets, many of which were subsequently printed in *Dagny*.

Just as she was about to embark on her teaching career, her father died and, consequently, Mårbacka and its contents were sold off at auction. She had now lost two of the most crucial figures from her childhood (her grandmother being the other). Although extremely distressed by these events, she became more determined to finish *Berling*. In 1885, she began working at the Landskrona High School for Girls. One of her pupils, Anna Clara, later recalled, 'I know no teacher who tried so hard as she to show us life as it really is.'[3] Her students were always convinced that she would become famous. Selma was a devoted teacher, concentrating on her work, and giving scant attention to her own personal life. Together with some of her colleagues, she formed an informal social circle which held evenings of stories and music. The members of this circle once asked each other to fill out a questionnaire. Selma's answers were revealing:

> 'What are your favourite qualities in a man?'
> 'Depth and earnestness.'
> 'What are your favourite qualities in a woman?'
> 'The same.'
> 'Your favourite occupation?'
> 'The study of character.'
> 'What do you consider the greatest happiness?'
> 'To believe in one's self.'[4]

In the spring of 1890, the women's magazine, *Idun*, held a novella competition. Eight days before the deadline, Selma decided to submit five chapters of *Gösta Berling's Saga* – but only three were actually finished. In between her school duties, she managed to complete the other two and sent off the manuscript. That November, she was announced as the winner. The Prize Committee declared, 'We were all carried away by the magic power of the mysterious story-teller.'[5] Many of her friends from college sent telegrams of 'Joyous Congratulations'.

Selma's success in the competition generated interest in the complete *Gösta Berling*, and so Sophie Adlersparre arranged for her to take a year off from teaching and stay with her friends, the Gumælin family, at Rocklunda to complete the work. The two-volume *Gösta Berling's Saga* was finally published in Sweden in December 1891 but did not have its greatest success until it was published in Denmark the following year. Swedish critics did not seem to know what to make of it. One, Oskar Levertin, said, 'It is the most curious brew of good and bad that I have ever seen. ... It is the style of heroic legend that is attained here.'[6] However, Denmark's top critic, Georg Brandes, championed the book and the breakthrough was made.

There is no question about Lagerlöf's talents as a skilful storyteller, but she also had the good fortune to be the right writer in the right country at the right time. In the late nineteenth century, Scandinavians, and Swedes in particular, had grown tired of the naturalistic style which had dominated their literature and were ready for a change in direction: a 'neo-romantic' reaction against the prevailing trends. They were ready to shake off the gloom and *Gösta Berling* was not so much a breath of fresh air, as a winter thaw. Readers were crying out for the work of a born storyteller, who combined the essential human qualities of humour, goodwill and compassion. Years later, the artist Carl Larsson, whose portrait of Selma hangs in the National Museum, Stockholm, said of her, 'I shudder to think what would have become of us in these dreadful times if we had not had that blessed woman.'[7]

In 1917 Selma approached the director Victor Seastrom and producer Svenska Bio to see if they would be interested in making films out of her books. A seven-year contract was signed, agreeing to shoot one film each year. However, initially they passed on *Berling* because Bio would not agree to provide enough money for such an epic. Not long after this, he left for Hollywood, and the director Mauritz Stiller decided to make the film in Sweden. Stiller's protégée, Greta Garbo, played one of Berling's two great loves, the young Countess Elizabeth Dohna. The book had been a childhood favourite of Garbo's and she regarded its creator as a heroine and a great example for women. Stiller and his writer Ragnar Hylten-Cavallius condensed the two volumes of stories into a four-hour film, improvising some of the scenes during filming.

The premiere of the first part of *Gösta Berling's Saga* was screened on 10 March 1924, in the Roda Kvarn Theatre in Stock-holm; part two was held a week later. It was an enormous hit, drawing dignitaries from all over Europe to its premieres and enjoy-ing official receptions attended by members of the Swedish Royal family. But Selma was reportedly unhappy with the adaptation of her writing, believing it to be cheap and sensational. To prevent her airing her views in public, Stiller allegedly got Selma drunk at the receptions and then made sure she was whisked off home. The film was not a critical success but Garbo's performance was: the burghers of Stockholm queued round the block to see the film.

Mauritz Stiller also filmed Selma's book, *The Treasure* (released as *Sir Arne's Treasure*), the story of three Scots mercen-aries in the army of Johan III of Sweden who take revenge on the man who betrayed them. Altogether, eleven films were made from Selma's books, not all of them as successful as *Berling*, which was also adapted for the stage in Sweden. The popularity of the tale of her likeable reprobate never waned over the years. It was eventually translated into thirty languages and, in 1940, topped a poll of the ten most popular novels in Sweden in the Stockholm newspaper, *Svenska Dagbladet*.

It was an intrinsic part of Swedish culture to encourage travel to other countries; indeed, it was regarded as an essential part of education. In 1895, Selma received the Royal Travelling Scholarship from King Oskar and Prince Eugen. After she gave up teaching in 1897, she and her mother went to live in Falun, where she was based for the next ten years. But she had been bitten by the late-nineteenth-century travel bug and, consequently, spent much of the next fifteen years roving from country to country. In her first year, she went to Italy, Switzerland, Germany, Belgium and Sicily. From 1898 to 1900, she returned to some of these countries and also added France, Holland, Egypt, Palestine, Turkey and Greece to her itinerary. From 1903 to 1912, more new countries were visited, including England, Bosnia, Finland, Denmark, Norway and Austria.

The woman at her side during these years was the writer Sophie Elkan, whom she had met in 1894. Born Sophie Saloman, of Jewish heritage, in Gothenburg in 1853, Elkan was the young, upper-class, cultured widow of a Stockholm music-dealer who had died in 1879. She began her literary career after his death, translating works edited by her brother. Her early novels were written under the Flemish pseudonym 'Rust, Roest' – literally, 'If I rest, I rust' – but her most popular work, *John Hall, the Millionaire-Pauper: A Tale of Old Gothenburg*, was published under her own name.

The two women formed an immediate bond; they spent the Easter of 1894 at the home of Sophie's uncle, and were together for most of the next twenty-five years. In addition to their years of foreign travel, they lived most of the time in Sweden, and Selma was equally welcome in the homes of Sophie's friends. When Sophie died in 1921, Selma delivered a touching oration at her graveside.

Selma had two other close relationships with women. One was Valborg Olander, an expert on the teaching of the Swedish language. The two met at a formal reception in 1897 for Selma when she moved to Falun. Valborg gave Selma invaluable help with manuscript copying, annotations and other tasks. Another intimate friend was the writer Anna Hamilton-Geete. In a book of 'personal reminiscences', she described Selma thus: 'She was pale – her eyes dim and absent-looking, her whole countenance wore an often moving expression of pathos and calm endurance.'[8]

Despite her many lengthy expeditions abroad, Selma Lagerlöf's literary output was prolific and diverse. Her travels themselves inspired some of her most popular works: Sicily provided the setting for *Miracles of Antichrist* (1897) and in Palestine she found the material for her two volumes of *Jerusalem* (1902). In 1899, Selma and Sophie visited Palestine to see a group of Swedish settlers from Dalecarlia who had emigrated to the Holy Land, under the influence of a revivalist from Chicago, and were now living with a colony of Americans in Jerusalem. The books were based on the Dalecarlians' experiences and centred on the character, Ingmar Ingmarsson, a taciturn fellow who pronounced, 'We Ingmarssons are noted for getting what we want.'[9] Interestingly, when her biographer Hanna Larsen asked Selma if she ever put herself into her characters, she replied, 'Yes, to some extent, more in the men than the women – Ingmar Ingmarsson, that drudge. ...'[10]

But it was, inevitably, the stories she had heard at Mårbacka that proved her greatest inspiration. She drew on them but eschewed the 'fairy-story' trappings of the form, successfully combining the supernatural with everyday life. The results included *Invisible Links* (1894), a collection of old Swedish folk-tales; *The Queens of Kungahalla* (1899), traditional stories of Viking raids and wars, as seen through a woman's eyes; and *Christ Legends* (1904), reworkings of old and new legends of Christ. *The Emperor of Portugallia* (1914) was a *Silas Marner*-like story of Jan, a simple man and his beloved daughter, Glory Goldie Sunnycastle, who is forced to leave home and sell herself on the streets of Stockholm. The trilogy, *The Rings of the Löwenskolds* (1925), chronicled the life of a female aristocrat living in the Napoleonic era.

In *Liljecrona's Home* (1911), the main character (based on Selma's grandfather, Daniel) was a violinist who had been one of Gösta Berling's cronies. The book itself was written while she and Sophie were getting ready to travel to Italy. Her Swedish publisher, Karl Otto Bonnier, was not happy with it and asked her to rewrite the ending. She did this en route to Italy, during a short stopover in Munich. Bonnier was happier with the new version but her partner was apparently less impressed: 'Sophie thinks my book is unimportant; I notice it although she does not say so in so many words.'[11] But she resolutely turned the other cheek: 'She is nearly always wrong in her opinion about my books.'[12]

Several main themes reoccur through her work. The need for travel and adventure is prominent, but always with the goal of having a secure, happy home life to return to. And, like Charles Dickens, Christmas was also a favourite theme. *Gösta Berling* begins and ends on Christmas Eve; *Liljecrona's Home* starts on a Christmas morning; plus, of course, the *Christ Legends*. The other important element in her works was love, an animating force beyond simple romantic desire. Her books were imbued with a love of country, of Mårbacka and her family (especially her father), of Värmland and its people. There was also her desire for international peace and unity, a hunger to embrace other countries and cultures and a concern for the welfare of humanity.

Her childhood on the farm was also the subject of several volumes, including *Mårbacka* (1922), *Memories of My Childhood* (1930) and *The Diary of Selma Lagerlöf* (1932). In 1906, the

Swedish school authorities commissioned her to write a book for children, as part of their efforts to keep alive the tradition of Swedish folklore. The results were two charming books, *The Wonderful Adventures of Nils* and *The Further Adventures of Nils*, featuring a Tom Thumb figure who rides across Sweden on the backs of wild geese. They eventually became two of the world's most popular, most translated children's books. Oskar Levertin declared, 'She has the eyes of a child and the heart of a child.'[13]

The First World War was a disturbing, unsettling experience for her. She had a horror of war and felt it imperative that women should do all they could to stop it. During the war she encouraged friends in Sweden to take in refugee children from warring countries. In 1915, she was involved in Polish relief work. After the war had ended, she helped to produce a series of fund-raising publications to aid prisoners in Siberia and the Red Cross. Her literary responses to war included *The Outcasts* (1918), the story of Sven Elverson, ostracized because he was rumoured to have eaten human flesh, and his eventual reacceptance into the community; and *Trolls and Men* (1915 and 1921), a collection of short stories influenced by the war.

She was always modest about her achievements. When *Mårbacka* proved popular, she commented, 'I am still amazed that my own countrymen are so captivated by it.'[14] Composer Ethel Smyth once asked Selma if she would write librettos for her. Selma replied:

> How glad I should be if I could say to you: 'Take this or that out of my works; it should make a good libretto!' But alas! I have not been able to find anything. You see I am not a dramatist and cannot see with such a one's eyes. It may perhaps help you to know that one of my books, 'Herr Arnes Schatz' has been dramatised by Gerhardt Hauptmann. Could you not write to him and ask him if there is something in his play to make music about?[15]

Years later, when Christopher St John was sorting through Smyth's manuscripts, she found a libretto called *John Arne's Treasure*.

Although Selma Lagerlöf eschewed syrupy sentimentality,

there was one significant event in her life that could have come straight out of a fairy-tale: in 1908, the house at Mårbacka was put up for sale and its most famous daughter was able to buy it back. She had it altered to make room for a proper study and library and spent the summers there. In 1910, she managed to buy back the entire estate, complete with sawmill and livestock. From 1919, she lived there all year round. The house and garden were restored to their former glory. As well as Mårbacka's herds of prize cows, the farm also produced a 'Mårbacka' breakfast cereal. On Christmas Eve, Selma would hold a party for all the estate's tenants and employees. Many visitors came to see both her and the inspirational landscape for so much of her work: critics, school parties and groups of Boy Scouts. She immersed herself in the local community again, donating money for road improvements and the construction of a new canal. She established a 'Gösta Berling' fund for old and needy women writers by donating her entire earnings from the *Berling* film.

From 1911, she was active in the suffrage society of Falun; she had always believed that better education and employment opportunities would revolutionize the position of unmarried women. In *Invisible Links*, one story, 'Mamselle Fredrika', describes a Mass held to celebrate the life and work of Fredrika Bremer, Sweden's first feminist, and her efforts for unmarried women: 'And a voice said: "Sisters, sisters! We were the neglected ones at the feast, the unthanked servants of the home."'[16]

Although she twice refused to stand for the Riksdag (Swedish Parliament), she was always ready to contribute whatever she could to furthering the advancement of women around the world. In 1911, at the Sixth Convention of the International Women's Suffrage Alliance, held at the Stockholm Opera House, she gave her first-ever public speech on women's suffrage. The basic thrust of her speech, 'Home and State', was that women had created the Home, man had created the State, and while women and men created homes together, men created states alone – which explains why they were generally no good. 'The great masterpiece, the good State, will be created by man when, in all seriousness, he takes woman as his helper.'[17]

She was always interested to learn what progress women in

other countries were making. One of Selma's main translators was an American writer, Velma Swanston Howard. At their first meeting, Howard recalled: 'She was eager to know about American women. She admired their freedom, vivacity, initiative.'[18] By then, she had become 'Dr Lagerlöf' – courtesy of honorary doctorates from the University of Upsala and other educational institutions – and, in 1909, was the first female recipient of the Nobel Prize for Literature. At the presentation in Stockholm she made a modest and moving speech, thanking her parents, the people of Värmland and her readers and critics: 'They have had such a beautiful faith in me that they have dared to distinguish me before the whole world.'[19] She paid homage to her father in the speech in the form of an imaginary conversation, in which she tells him of her achievements and her new honour. As well as being the first woman to receive the Nobel Prize for Literature, she was also the first woman to be given the Swedish Academy's Gold Medal (in 1904) and, in 1914, was made the first female member of the Academy itself.

In 1908, the year of her jubilee, there were nation-wide celebrations; on her seventieth birthday, these became international. She received a thousand congratulatory telegrams and numerous deputations from Swedish organizations and representatives of Church and state. On the evening of her birthday, a performance of the opera *I Cavalieri di Ekebu* by Riccardo Zandonai, based on *Gösta Berling*, was given in her honour, together with a banquet afterwards at the Grand Hotel in Stockholm.

Selma Lagerlöf died at her birthplace on 16 March 1940, aged eighty-one. The only other Swedish woman more famous and celebrated was the reclusive film star who had been such an admirer: Greta Garbo. Her obituary in *The Times* called her 'the greatest of contemporary Swedish writers'. It continued, 'Through all the developments in the life of her country Selma Lagerlöf held on her way with a stalwart faith, a large heart, and a wise and noble mind.'[20] In the preface to a biography of Lagerlöf, the ubiquitous Vita Sackville-West observed, 'Selma Lagerlöf, like a skilled juggler, has contrived over a respect-worthy number of years to spin her two plates; the plates of realism and of fantasy',[21] and considered her style to be that of 'a poet writing in prose'.[22] Importantly, she also observed, 'She writes always as a woman: not one of her books could have been written by a man. Her art is essentially feminine, not masculine, yet without the slightest consciousness of sex.'[23]

Almost single-handedly, Selman Lagerlöf's 'plate-spinning' changed the face of nineteenth-century Scandinavian literature by drawing on the very roots of its people. In the process, she created the most unlikely mythical figure of Värmland's history: herself.

Notes

1. F. S. de Vrieza, *Fact and Fiction in the Autobiographical Work of Selma Lagerlöf* (Assen, Van Gorum & Co., 1958), p. 36.
2. Walter A. Berendsohn, *Selma Lagerlöf: Her Life and Work* (London, Nicholson & Watson, 1931), p. 9.
3. *Ibid.*, p. 15.
4. *Ibid.*, p. 17.
5. *Ibid.*, p. 21.
6. Alrik Gustefson, *Six Scandinavian Novelists* (New York, Princeton, 1940), p. 186.
7. Marius Kristiansen, *Selma Lagerlöf* (H. A. Larsen, 1936), p. 48.
8. Berendsohn, *Life and Work*, p. 25.
9. Kristiansen, *Selma Lagerlöf*, p. 63.
10. *Ibid.*
11. de Vrieza, *Fact and Fiction*, p. 22.
12. *Ibid.*, p. 27.
13. Berendsohn, *Life and Work*, p. xviii.
14. de Vrieza, *Fact and Fiction*, p. 18.
15. Christopher St John, *Ethel Smyth: A Biography* (London, Longmans, 1959), p. 133.
16. Selma Lagerlöf, *Invisible Links*, p. 101.
17. *Tracts Relating to Women 1907–13* (London, International Women's Suffrage Alliance, 1913), p. 11.
18. Berendsohn, *Life and Work*, p. 83.
19. Gustefson, *Scandinavian Novelists*, p. 224.
20. *The Times*, 18 March 1940.
21. Berendsohn, *Life and Work*, p. v.
22. *Ibid.*, p. viii.
23. *Ibid.*, p. x.

Frances Power Cobbe

AND now, a history quiz. Who made the following radical statements about the contemporary validity of some carved-in-granite theological beliefs?

The tabernacle where our fathers worshipped has visibly been lifted up, and no longer stands on its old ground; and with it the innermost shrines of our religion are all moved from their resting place.

We doubt many things which our fathers never doubted; and look on things which they accepted with unquestioning confidence, as, at the very best, beset with difficulties.

To love God is to love his creatures, even the poorest and meanest – even the brutes. ... Before His eyes we all admit that there must be equality.

Well, it certainly wasn't the Pope or Mary Whitehouse. Could it have been, perhaps, the Bishop of Durham, infamous rattler of the Church's cage? Mother Teresa of Calcutta? Or maybe the Sisters of Perpetual Indulgence? In fact, these rather prophetic statements are taken from a book written over 130 years ago by a complex, rather contradictory Anglo-Irish woman who, after years chained to her intellectually repressive family, became one of the most pioneering and radical philosophers and activists of her time.

Frances Power Cobbe was born on 14 December 1822, the only daughter of Charles and Frances Conway Power Cobbe, a landowning, strict Protestant Anglo-Irish family; there were already four sons. She credited her parents with more of her physical attributes than her mental capabilities: 'From them I have inherited a physical frame which, however defective even to the verge of grotesqueness from the aesthetic point of view, has been, as regards health and energy, a source of endless enjoyment to me.'[1]

Her home life at Newbridge House, County Dublin, was comfortable but lonely. She enjoyed the best of everything – food, animals, servants – but there were no other children her age to play with and her mother was incapacitated because of inappropriate treatment given to what had started out as a minor ankle injury. Frances later recalled with sadness that 'she was never once able in all her life to take a walk with me'.[2]

When the weather was bad, she would spend her days in the library. During the holidays, though, her many cousins would come to stay at Newbridge. At Christmas time, there was usually a family gathering of over twenty people. Naturally, since it was one of the few occasions when there were other children around, it was Frances's favourite time of the year.

There is nothing to suggest that she felt particularly rooted to her homeland or had any great sense of Irish identity. Once she was asked by an MP, 'What do you know about Ireland?'; she replied, 'Simply that the first 36 years of my life were spent there.'[3] She was, however, aware of the poverty endured by the Irish field labourers and of the prevalence and wealth of the Protestant gentry. Charles Power Cobbe was not a typical country squire, either: during the potato famine, he made sure his estate's tenants had enough to eat – one reason, perhaps, why the Cobbes were not an integral part of Dublin society.

In 1836, Frances was sent to a girls' boarding school in Brighton. At that time the seaside town was heaving with such establishments; there were believed to be at least a hundred. Frances hated the school and always wrote of it in the most disparaging terms. She scorned the fact that music and dancing were at the top of the curriculum and was horrified that a Religious Studies lesson on fasting advocated the practice on the basis that 'it would be good for our souls AND OUR FIGURES!'[4] This seemed to fit in well with her father's idea of how a girl should be educated, since he was happy for Frances to have music lessons but did not want her to learn Latin. No doubt her experiences at this school led to her becoming so concerned about women's education.

Two years later, she returned to Newbridge and was given the responsibility of running the household: planning menus, paying the servants' wages, inspecting the larders and kitchens. She was to do this for the next twenty years. Paradoxically, she always claimed to have enjoyed her position and duties: 'The woman's destiny which God has allotted to me has been, I do not question, the best and happiest for me.'[5] And yet she was well aware of the limitations of that destiny. She reflected that, for a woman of her class, 'housekeeping and needlework were her only fitting pursuits. The one natural ambition of her life was supposed to be a "suitable" marriage; study of any sort was disapproved'.[6]

While she may not have questioned this conventional wisdom to any great extent, she was, by this time, having serious doubts about another: her Protestant faith. These doubts had begun when she was eleven, as she explained: 'The first question which ever arose in my mind was concerning the miracle of the Loaves and Fishes. What was done to them? Did the fish grow and grow as they were eaten and broken?'[7]

During her time at boarding school, the doubts intensified, particularly about the miracles allegedly performed by Jesus. It might seem ridiculous to us now but, at that time, for a dyed-in-the-wool Evangelical Protestant girl, this was no laughing matter and Frances summed up her dilemma thus:

> On the one hand I had the choice to accept a whole mass of dogmas against which my reason and conscience rebelled; on the other, to abandon those dogmas and strive no more to believe the incredible, or to revere what I instinctively condemned.[8]

Finally, after four years of wrestling with her conscience, she declared, 'I definitely disbelieved in human immortality and in a supernatural revelation. I was, in fact, precisely – an Agnostic.'[9] But she had not jettisoned the last vestiges of her beliefs; instead, she had undergone a thorough re-evaluation of what God should really have represented:

> I asked myself, 'Can I not rise once more, conquer my faults, and live up to my own idea of what is right and good.' I simply addressed Him as the Lord of conscience ... of dogmatical Christianity there was never any more.[10]

She kept these supposedly heretical thoughts to herself, going through the motions at family prayers and services.

In 1847, her mother died, leaving her only daughter bereft with grief and more isolated than ever. It was a loss Frances never really came to terms with. In her old age, she wrote sadly and movingly of her mother: 'Almost her last words were to tell me I had been "the pride and joy" of her life.'[11] The 'pride and joy' had now become entirely responsible for running the family home – without the prospect of ever inheriting it.

When, eventually, she revealed her new religious views to her father, his response was entirely what you would expect from a Protestant patriarch – he packed her off to live with one of her brothers on his farm in Donegal. She was exiled there for nearly ten months, 'not knowing whether I should ever be permitted to return home and rather expecting to be disinherited'.[12] She did, however, begin to formulate her new thoughts into an 'Essay on True Religion'.

On her return to Newbridge, she resumed the role of housekeeper but was excused from attending church or family prayers. For the next eight years, Frances Power Cobbe lived her life with a curious combination of acceptance and suppressed rebelliousness. She later admitted that those years 'though mentally very lonely, were far from unhappy'.[13]

When she was thirty, she became extremely ill with a near-fatal bout of bronchitis. She was sent to convalesce in Devon and used the time to expand her essay. This eventually became *The Theory of Intuitive Morals* and was published anonymously in 1855. It was well received critically: one reviewer commented, 'It is a most noble performance, the work of a masculine and lofty mind.'[14] However, when it began to emerge that the author, though certainly no shrinking violet, might not be quite as masculine as they had imagined, the critics viewed it less favourably.

During the next ten years, she honed and refined her beliefs and, in 1864, published *Broken Lights*, her definitive book on the failings of modern religion and her belief in the new 'Theism' which she had embraced. This, she explained,

> will assert not only the Unity and Eternity and Wisdom and Justice of God, but above all that one great attribute which is our principal concern, HIS GOODNESS. Here lies the essence of Theism – its practical difference from every other creed in the world. Every religion which has ever existed calls God 'good' – applies pompous epithets of moral honour to His nature.[15]

She then set out Theism's three principles: 'the ABSOLUTE GOODNESS OF GOD; the FINAL SALVATION OF EVERY CREATED SOUL; and the DIVINE AUTHORITY OF CON-SCIENCE – are the obvious fundamental canons of the Faith of the Future'.[16] And, in what was a remarkably radical statement for the times, she asserted,

> If we are to climb up to God, we must bear our brethren along with us. We hear of 'the supreme Caucasian mind' and of miserable 'Niggers'; and of convicts and criminals who ought to be crushed like venomous reptiles under the heel of society without pity or hesitation. The religion that will leave men to speak and feel like this will never be, and *ought* never to be the religion of the world.[17]

There was one chink in her liberal armour, however: anti-Semitism. She saw Jews as the bane of Irish farmers, imagining that they would foreclose on those who had borrowed money from them. 'We shall see the Jews flocking over to Ireland', she predicted; when she was writing her autobiography, she declared, 'I am informed that the Jews have settled down in Ireland like seagulls on the land after a storm'.[18] Whatever else Ireland has become in the intervening years, it is certainly not a Jewish settlement.

When her father died in 1857, she was at last free of her duties, but she also became homeless when her eldest brother and his wife were installed as the new owners. Moreover, her father had left her an annuity of a mere £200 per year – less than she had received while living at home. Although she admitted 'leaving Newbridge was the worst wrench of my life',[19] she readily accepted her poverty in exchange for her new-found freedom. In the true fashion of a Victorian lady, she embarked on a marathon journey, which took her eleven months. Her itinerary included Rome, Paris, Venice, Milan, Athens, Corfu, Lebanon and Jordan. 'I had taken my year's pilgrimage as a sort of conclusion to my self-education',[20] she explained.

During her time in Italy, she met some equally remarkable women who confirmed that her place was at the writing table, rather than the kitchen table. These included the American actress Charlotte Cushman, writer Mary Somerville, the sculptor Harriet Hosmer and, briefly, Rosa Bonheur. Most of the women she met in this 'colony' had enjoyed longstanding relationships with other women, something she envied them.

She returned to England in the autumn of 1858, homeless and jobless. By November, however, her friend, Harriet St Leger, had made arrangements for her to go to Bristol to join Mary Carpenter at her Red Lodge Reformatory and Ragged School. Carpenter was, according to Frances, 'not only the guardian and teacher of the poor young waifs and strays ... she was also their unwearied advocate with one government after another'.[21]

The Red Lodge Reformatory looked after fifty girls, aged between ten and fifteen. The days were full, the work demanding and Frances, used to multi-course meals with a tasty bill-of-fare, found Carpenter's plain offerings not at all to her liking. On one occasion, when she complained about the lack of vegetables, Carpenter presented her with a plate containing six small radishes. Nonetheless, Frances seemed able to put her own perceived hardships into perspective and was as committed to the girls' welfare as her abstemious colleague. She pledged, 'Let us make the [workhouse] girls, first safe; then as happy as we can.'[22] She also shared Carpenter's concern about housing for the poor in urban centres.

It has been suggested that, in Mary Carpenter, Frances

thought she had found her sought-after lifelong companion. If so, then she was disappointed. Carpenter told her, 'My work and my cause require and must have the devotion of all my heart and soul and strength. I thank you much for your love, and know that you think much better of me than I deserve.'[23] Frances sadly mused, 'She would have liked me better if I had been a delinquent.'[24]

She left Bristol in 1859 and decided to take up journalism full time. Although she had already done some writing, it was primarily her health that forced her into this decision. Uncannily, she suffered the same fate as her mother: a simple sprained ankle was incorrectly treated by a doctor and, as a result, she was hardly able to walk for four years. Little wonder that, years later, while walking up a mountain in Wales with a friend, she declared 'Hang the Doctors!'

In 1860, during one of her frequent excursions to Italy, she met Mary Lloyd, a friend of Charlotte Cushman's. Lloyd was studying sculpture in Rome. When Frances returned to the city in 1862, Lloyd was still there. But when she returned to England, Mary went with her. A woman of inherited means, Mary Lloyd immediately bought a house for the two of them in Hanover Square, London, and Frances reflected, 'My lonely wanderings were over'.[25] As, indeed, were the career aspirations of Mary Lloyd. From this time onwards, it was Frances's work which took precedence in the relationship. The pair also remained in London for many years, against the wishes of Mary, who longed to live in her home in Wales, which they used for holidays. There is no doubt that Frances knew what a prize Mary was, as is evident in a passionate poem she wrote to her in 1873:

> *Friend of my life! Whene'er my eyes*
> *Rest with sudden, glad surprise*
> *On Nature's scenes of earth and air*
> *Sublimely grand, or sweetly fair,*
> > *I want you, Mary.*

> *And when the winter nights come round*
> *to our 'ain fireside' cheerly bound*
> *With our dear Rembrandt Girl, so brown,*

Smiling serenely on us down
                    I want you, Mary.

Hereafter, when slow ebbs the tide,
And age drains out my strength and pride
And dim-grown eyes and trembling hand
No longer list my soul's command
                    I'll want you, Mary.

In joy and grief, in good and ill,
Friend of my heart! I need you still;
My Playmate, Friend, Companion, Love,
To dwell with here, to clasp above
                    I want you, Mary.

For O! if past the gates of Death
To me the Unseen Openeth
Immortal joys to angels given
Upon the holy heights of Heaven
                    I'll want you, Mary!

In her autobiography, she wrote of her gratitude for 'two precious benedictions in life; – in my youth, a perfect Mother, in my later years, a perfect Friend'.[26]

Her journalistic career began with a series of travel articles on Rome, Cairo and Athens and Jerusalem for *Fraser's Magazine*, run by a Mr Froude, one of her brother's friends from Oxford. For one year, she was the Rome correspondent for the *Daily News*. She also wrote for the *Spectator*, *The Economist*, *Macmillan's Magazine* and the *Quarterly Review*. She loved her work: 'I always pitied the clerks for their dull monotonous, ugly work, as compared with mine,' she said.[27]

In 1868, she joined a new publication, the *Echo*, Britain's first halfpenny paper. In the next thirteen years, she wrote over a thousand leading articles for them, including many on poverty. She left them to join the *Standard* but resigned after a pro-vivisection article appeared in the paper. In fact, her commitment to the anti-vivisection campaign seriously affected her career; after she helped form the Victoria Street Society, she earned no more than £100 a year and, from 1882 until 1894, this dropped to £20.

However, until this time she enjoyed life to the full. Summers were spent at the house in Wales, and there were occasional visits to her brothers in Ireland. The rest of the time, she had a busy social life. She estimated that during the twenty years she and Mary lived in London, she went to around two thousand dinners. On one such occasion, at a friend's house in Regent's Park, she was introduced to the writer Charles Kingsley who, of course, shared her concern for poor and underprivileged children. Still crippled and on crutches, she was announced by a servant as 'Miss Cobble'. She loudly corrected this, to 'No! Miss *Hobble*!',[28] and Kingsley, much amused, rose to help 'Miss Hobble-Cobble' to the table. Other friends in London included the philosopher John Stuart Mill, author of *Subjection of Women* and Dr Elizabeth Garrett, subject of a poem written by Frances in her honour:

> *At the end of day, when all is done,*
> *And Woman's battle fought and won,*
> *Honour will aye be paid to one*
> *Who erst called foremost in the van*
>
> *Excelsior!*

But it was not all dinner parties and ditties: Frances threw herself into a number of organizations concerned with political and social reform. She became involved in the Kensington Discussion Society, was elected a member of the Married Women's Property Committee and, briefly, served on the Executive Committee of the London National Society for Women's Suffrage. She was a regular contributor to the *Women's Suffrage Journal*. She also joined the Primrose League, an organization which sought to increase support for the Conservative Party at grass-roots level, especially among women; apparently, she thought support for the League would further the cause of women's suffrage.

As Frances admitted, she had not become an advocate of women's rights until her years in Bristol, where she was affected by the suffering of the women and girls she worked with, rather than her own experiences: 'such wrongs as these have inspired me with the persistent resolution to do everything in my power to protect the property, the persons and the parental rights of women',[29] she explained. But there seemed to be limits to her feminism. She felt that 'women en masse are by no means the intellectual equals of men en masse; – and whether this inequality arises from irremediable causes or from alterable circumstances of education and heredity, is not worth debating'.[30] Of course, this sort of dismissive attitude may simply have been a form of self-protection – any serious contemplation of the deep-rooted causes of women's inequality, particularly regarding the questions of inheritances and education for daughters, would have emphasized quite clearly and painfully how badly she had fared at the hands of her father and brothers.

She did, however, accept that if a woman's lot was to improve, then men had to contribute. In 1876, she addressed a women's suffrage meeting at St George's Hall, London. In her speech, she declared:

> With all my soul, I believe that the interests of women are really the interests of men; and that it is no more the interest of men that women should be wronged, than it is for the good of my right hand that my left should be maimed.[31]

By this time, of course, she had become overwhelmingly involved in the fight to outlaw an institutionalized form of maiming carried out by many hands, left and right, male and female: vivisection.

She had considered the issue when she was sixteen: concerned that impaling live fish on hooks for sport might not exactly be humane she resolved to give up fishing. But it was not until 1863, when she read newspaper reports of operations carried out on live horses at veterinary schools in France, that she put pen to paper and wrote an article called 'The Rights of Man and the Claims of Brutes' for *Fraser's Magazine*. And, as synchronicity dictates, while on holiday in Italy shortly after, she heard of similar experiments carried out there on cats.

She was finally spurred into action in 1874, when it was

disclosed that experiments on live animals were to be carried out at a medical congress in Norwich. The RSPCA took legal action against the organizers and began to solicit support among the medical profession. A Mrs Luther Holden, wife of the senior surgeon at St Bartholomew's Hospital in London, asked Frances's advice about what could be done to strengthen the law. Frances promptly drew up a draft document on the subject; petitions were organized and letters written to politicians, but a draft bill of 1875 to prohibit vivisection failed to muster enough support. The government set up a Royal Commission on Vivisection but its report was inconclusive. At this juncture, Frances decided to form a campaigning organization. She wrote to Lord Shaftesbury and the Archbishop of York, who agreed to join up, as did Cardinal Manning, and the Victoria Street Society for the Protection of Animals was established.

The Society held its inaugural meeting in London on 2 December 1875; its main objective was 'to obtain the greatest possible protection for animals liable to vivisection'.[32] Anti-vivisectionists, explained Frances, were sceptical about the alleged benefits of animal experiments: 'We question the reality of those benefits altogether ... they are of no appreciable weight compared to the certain moral injury done to the community by the sanctions of cruelty.'[33]

There was never any question of her own commitment. She resolved 'never to go to bed at night leaving a stone unturned which might help to stop Vivisection'.[34] In the next fifteen years, she wrote 320 books, pamphlets and leaflets on vivisection. She was the Society's joint secretary and editor of its magazine, *The Zoophilist*, until she moved to Wales in 1884. Out of all her diverse activities, her work against vivisection was, for her, the most important: 'When I laboured in former years with Mary Carpenter to reform young thieves, I do not think I worked more directly for the good of human beings than when I now labour to stop both young and old vivisectors in their course of cruelty.'[35] She fell out with many friends over the issue (although she never allowed the subject to be raised at the dinner table) and gradually found herself less welcome in certain social circles.

In 1884, *The Vivisectors' Directory* was published, listing all licensed vivisectors in Britain. In its preface, Frances declared:

> The Directory is a mere dry Register. ... If these should
> happen to convey most damning accusations, it is the Vivi-
> sectors themselves who have registered their own offences.
> We have before us in this small Directory a record of agonies
> before which the brain grows dizzy and the heart sick.

She was not exaggerating: the practitioners listed in the booklet
regularly had animals baked, electrocuted, poisoned, cut open and
injected.

The Society lobbied the British government for years. In
1876, Frances had a meeting with Prime Minister William
Gladstone after she had sent him a copy of an article on vivisection.
He promised to support any legislation to outlaw vivisection and,
with high hopes, a deputation from the Society went to see Home
Office ministers. The same year, a draft bill, the Vivisection Act,
was read in Parliament; it called for no experiments whatsoever to
be carried out on dogs, cats or horses. Unfortunately, as is often the
way with private members' bills, it was amended and modified until
it allowed for legal control of experiments, thus 'no longer protect-
ing vivisected animals from torture but vivisectors from prosecution'.[36] For Frances, it was a shattering blow, from which she
was still smarting twenty years later: 'The world has never seemed
to me quite the same since that dreadful time. Justice and Mercy
seemed to have gone from the earth.'[37]

Eventually, the Society decided to abandon its demand for
the total prohibition of experiments on animals. Frances was ve-
hemently against this resolution but could not prevent it being
passed at a committee meeting in 1898. She resigned from the
Society and set up the British Society for the Abolition of Vivisection. Despite this rather bitter parting of the ways, the Victoria
Street Society arranged for her to receive an annuity of £100, in
recognition of her years of dedicated campaigning and, in addition,
a sizeable lump sum from a legacy left to the Society by a supporter
of their work.

She saw many links between the struggles for women's
rights and animal rights. In her view, women and animals were
both subject to the brutality and power of doctors, scientists and
other men. In an article written in 1878 for the *Contemporary*

Review on the acceptance of domestic violence, entitled 'Wife Torture in England', she called for reformation of the Matrimonial Causes Act. This would enable women to gain legal separation from their violent husbands. She, however, rejected another proposed solution to the problem: that the men should be flogged. Years later, she received a letter which described how one particular woman, under the new Matrimonial Causes Act, had finally been rescued from her brutal husband. She was told, 'We live wider lives and better for your presence. This! that poor battered, bruised women are safer.' Even in this, her thoughts were never far from animals: 'If I could hear before I die that I had been able to do as much for tortured brutes, I should say "Nunc Dimittis" and wish no more.'[38]

In 1884, she and Mary left London for good and moved to Hengwrt in Wales. She explained, 'The strain of London life had become too great for me and advancing years and narrowed income together counselled retreat in good time.'[39] Mary, of course, had been advocating such a move for many years. Although life was not as hectic as it had been in London, Frances continued to write, campaign, lecture and socialize.

But in 1898 came the double blow of the split with the Victoria Street Society and, more significantly, Mary's death. As she lay dying, Mary urged her partner to continue her fight against vivisection. Frances said she died 'calmly and bravely resting on my arm and telling me we should not long be separated'.[40] Her friend, Blanche Atkinson, remembered that

> the sorrow of Miss Lloyd's death changed the whole aspect of existence for Miss Cobbe. The joy of life had gone. It had been such a friendship as is rarely seen – perfect in love, sympathy and mutual understanding. To the very last she could never mention the name of 'my dear Mary' or of her own mother, without a break in her voice.[41]

Frances visited Mary's grave often, usually early in the morning, and particularly if she had problems. Being near to Mary, she believed, could help her solve them. But, as Blanche Atkinson explained, 'There was nothing morbid in her grief. She took the same keen interest as before in the daily affairs of life.'[42] Indeed she did. As well as continuing to campaign against vivisection, she had a convivial social life in her country home. She would go for drives in her horse-cart and held dinners and garden parties for her neighbours. She joined the Women's Liberal Federation and spoke out against the Boer War. However, as Blanche Atkinson said, 'The last years of her life were not as peacefully happy as one would have loved to paint them.'[43]

On her eightieth birthday, friends organized a congratulatory address, signed by English and American dignitaries, in recognition of her work on women's equality in education, poverty and animal rights. By this time, she was certainly in need of moral support. That summer, someone in a neighbouring village, who clearly did not approve of her radicalism, initiated a vindictive and malicious accusation: Frances Power Cobbe found herself charged with 'cruelly overdriving an old horse'. Blanche Atkinson wrote bitterly of the affair: 'It was pitiful! She had but a few months to live and this was what a little group of her enemies did to dark and embitter those few months!'[44] The charge, of course, was found to be groundless but, for an ailing old lady who had spent decades of her life fighting for better treatment of animals, it was especially upsetting and shocking.

On 4 April 1904, she went for a drive, wrote letters and had tea with a neighbour. The next morning, her maid found her dead in bed, although she had obviously been up – the shutters of her windows had been opened. She was buried next to Mary Lloyd in the churchyard at Llanelltyd. She once told Blanche Atkinson, 'Nobody must be sorry when that time comes, least of all those who love me.'[45]

She did not live long enough to see her dream of full suffrage for women come true, or the other advances which went far beyond her initial views on women's rights. These improvements would, of course, have delighted her but she would have been far from happy with the progress made on other issues close to her heart.

Her greatest wish was that 'long after I have passed away, mankind will have attained through it a recognition of our duties towards the lower animals'.[46] Although her pioneering work against vivisection has been carried on by organizations such as

Animal Aid, the British Union of Anti-Vivisectionists and even the Animal Liberation Front, she would have been horrified by the number of experiments still carried out on animals in Britain and elsewhere. Her dream of equality for 'even the poorest and meanest – even the brutes' is still a long way from reality.

Notes

1. Frances Power Cobbe, *Life of Frances Power Cobbe* (introd. Blanche Atkinson) (London, Swan, Sonnenschein, 1904), p. 3.
2. *Ibid.*, p. 33.
3. *Ibid.*, p. 445.
4. *Ibid.*, p. 66.
5. *Ibid.*, p. 5.
6. *Ibid.*, p. 170.
7. *Ibid.*, pp. 86–7.
8. *Ibid.*, p. 91.
9. *Ibid.*, p. 92.
10. *Ibid.*, p. 93.
11. *Ibid.*, p. 99.
12. *Ibid.*, p. 101.
13. *Ibid.*, p. 105.
14. *Ibid.*, p. 114.
15. Frances Power Cobbe, *Broken Lights* (London, Trubner and Co., 1864), p. 157.
16. *Ibid.*, p. 173.
17. *Ibid.*, pp. 185–6.
18. Cobbe, *Life*, p. 509.
19. *Ibid.*, p. 213.
20. *Ibid.*, p. 275.
21. *Ibid.*, p. 285.
22. *Ibid.*, p. 337.
23. Letter, 28 November 1859.
24. Jo Manton, *Mary Carpenter and the Children of the Streets* (London, Heinemann, 1976), p. 151.
25. Cobbe, *Life*, p. 396.
26. *Ibid.*, pp. 709–10.
27. *Ibid.*, p. 429.
28. *Ibid.*, p. 454.
29. *Ibid.*, p. 584.
30. *Ibid.*
31. Jane Lewis (ed.), *Before the Vote was Won* (London, Routledge & Kegan Paul, 1987), p. 265.

32. Cobbe, *Life*, p. 649.
33. *Ibid.*, pp. 665–6.
34. *Ibid.*, p. 647.
35. Jennie Chappell, *Women of Worth* (London, S. W. Partridge, 1908), p. 132.
36. Cobbe, *Life*, p. 653.
37. *Ibid.*, p. 654.
38. *Ibid.*, p. 599.
39. *Ibid.*, p. 695.
40. *Ibid.*, p. 710.
41. *Ibid.*, p. vi.
42. *Ibid.*, p. vii.
43. *Ibid.*, p. viii.
44. *Ibid.*, p. xiii.
45. *Ibid.*, p. xxii.
46. Chappell, *Women of Worth*, p. 132.

Dame Ethel Smyth

IN 1993 the seventy-fifth anniversary of British women being given the vote went largely unmarked, but one token effort was made: the BBC repeated the groundbreaking series, *Shoulder to Shoulder*, devised in 1974 by Midge Mackenzie, the late Georgia Brown and Verity Lambert. A laudable decision by the BBC; unfortunately, the programmes were transmitted after eleven o'clock on a Sunday evening – hardly 'peak viewing time'. But for those who remember the series, one of its most memorable features was the bold-as-brass, exuberant theme tune which, decades before, had stirred the suffragettes to greater acts of courage and conviction. It was written by one from among their own ranks, a woman who, in her *March of the Women*, virtually drew a musical self-portrait – England's finest female composer who, in her lifetime, knew all about her work being kept out of 'peak viewing time'.

Ethel Smyth was born in Sidcup, Kent, on 23 April 1858, to Major-General J. H. and Nina Smyth, after a ten-month pregnancy – something that Ethel herself took particular pride in, until she discovered feminism: '[I had heard] that such children are generally boys, and are always remarkable!'[1] She had five sisters and two brothers; the eldest three children had been born in India, where their father had been posted, and Ethel was the first to be born in England. The family lived in relative comfort in Sidcup Place in the town of Foots Cray, Kent.

General Smyth treated his children as if they were just another unruly regiment. He pinned a note on the nursery wall which read, 'If you have nothing pleasant to say hold your tongue.'[2] When Ethel was caught stealing a piece of barley sugar, he thrashed her with a 2½-foot-long knitting needle, threatening, 'The more noise you make the harder I'll hit you.'[3] The marks were still there a fortnight later. Other punishments included being shut in an empty room at the top of the house or in their father's darkened dressing-room. Once, when Ethel and her sister Mary were shut in there, they made a full-length effigy of him, complete with an inscription in pins that read, 'For dear Papa'.

The young Ethel developed some early passions for other girls: Ellinor B, a young woman in the church choir; and Ethel's cousin, Louie. She took a keen interest in people's love affairs and admitted that even then, 'love seemed to me the only thing that mattered; but nothing less than Keats's unquenchable flame of course'.[4]

In 1867, General Smyth was put in command of the Artillery at Aldershot in Hampshire and the family moved into a new home, Frimhurst, near Farnborougb. The Smyth children went to endless glamorous parties and balls. The boys were sent to elite public schools while the girls were taught by an endless stream of governesses. By now, Ethel had already started to compile her 'Book of Passions', which included names of over a hundred girls and women to whom, had she been a man, she would have proposed. Ethel admitted, 'From the first my most ardent sentiments were bestowed on members of my own sex.'[5] The only governess who appeared on the list was one Miss Hammond, but any passionate feelings came to an abrupt end when the unfortunate woman slipped on some ice and the hair, which Ethel had been so taken with, rolled off Hammond's head. The day Miss Hammond left Frimhurst for good, Ethel clung on to the back of her carriage, hissing, 'I know your chignon [wig] is false!' Another governess, a German woman, fared even worse: during the Franco-Prussian War, Ethel and her sisters would rush into her room in the mornings and relate gory details of fictional German defeats. Little wonder that governesses did not last long.

But one did eventually impress the twelve-year-old Ethel, a woman who had studied music at the Leipzig Conservatorium. From her, Ethel heard her first classical music and resolved that she, too, would study in Leipzig one day, although no one in her family took her intentions seriously. Her formal music lessons were given by a German tutor; Ethel began to write her own compositions and taught her sisters chants and hymns.

When she was eighteen, she visited a cousin in Ireland, where she met a young barrister called Willie Wilde. On the return boat trip, he introduced her to his brother – Oscar. At Holyhead, the weary travellers shared a cramped railway compartment, and Willie Wilde had to resort to sitting on a biscuit tin. At some stage in the journey, he declared his undying passion for Ethel, at which point the biscuit tin collapsed under him. Before they arrived in London, Ethel had somehow agreed to marry 'a man I was no more in love with than I was with the engine driver!'[6] Within a few weeks, however, she had managed to extricate herself from this arrangement.

Life at Frimhurst continued to revolve around a string of society balls, at which Ethel felt increasingly out of place as she pretended to flirt with the young bucks of the county. But in 1872, tragedy struck when John, the eldest son, was injured in a riding accident. The injuries turned out to be more serious than at first thought and, as a result of incorrect treatment, he became confined to a wheelchair and, consequently, died in 1875. That same year her father's command came to an end; he retired and bought Frimhurst. Although Ethel continued to show musical prowess, he was still against her Leipzig plan. Her parents argued almost daily over the issue and Ethel protested against her father's stubborness with some fairly tenacious behaviour of her own: she refused to go to church or to dinner parties, would not speak to anyone and locked herself in her room. Eventually, aided by the gentle persuasion of sympathetic family friends, the General relented and Ethel left for Leipzig in July 1877.

Once there, she was introduced to the cream of Leipzig society and was, by all accounts, a popular addition to their ranks. Sir George Henschel admired her musical talents and athletic prowess and later recalled, 'We all agreed that we had amongst us an extraordinarily commanding personality.'[7] She was introduced to Brahms, an early influence on her composing; the celebrated singer Livia Frege and Lili Wach, Mendelssohn's youngest daughter. Tchaikovsky thought her work showed a great deal of promise but (naturally) advised her not to be over-influenced by Brahms's works.

But by far the most important person she met in Leipzig was Elisabeth ('Lisl') von Herzogenberg. Apart from having a long, intense relationship with her, Ethel also became entangled with other members of Lisl's family. When Ethel observed, 'where elemental forces such as love, pride and jealousy are in play, the wild parabolas that human nature is capable of executing, defy calculation',[8] she inadvertently but accurately summed up the confused, emotional tangle that involved Lisl and, eventually, her sister and brother-in-law, Julia and Henry 'HB' Brewster.

But first, Lisl. She was twenty-nine and married when Ethel met her. Ethel, meanwhile, had been seeing a good deal of a Frau Dr Brockhaus who, she said, 'had been my all-in-all till Lisl appeared on the scene'.[9] Lisl's 'entrance' was signalled when Ethel collapsed with suspected palpitations (actually stress) at a party and she and Frau Brockhaus competed with each other to nurse her. Years later, Ethel confessed, 'I only half remember the battle fought over the corpse-like form in the bed. But Frau Brockhaus, a sensitive Hungarian, soon saw how matters stood and left the field to Lisl.'[10] Which actually suited her fine. When Lisl had to leave Leipzig for a fortnight, Ethel 'missed her so dreadfully that most nights my pillow was wet with tears'.[11] Ethel went back to England for a short period of convalescence but, with her father still bickering over money, she soon returned to Germany to live with the Herzogenbergs.

Ethel once admitted, 'If ever I worshipped a being on earth it was Lisl.'[12] No doubt – but she led Lisl a merry dance. She would have lengthy holidays in England, Italy and Switzerland, leaving the adored Lisl in Leipzig. She also seemed to be something of an emotional butterfly, bestowing her affection indiscriminately on a string of women. Although Lisl told her, 'still I enjoy somehow the idea of having to fight for you', it was obviously painful: 'if I loved you less how little I should suffer!', she wrote.[13] Lisl's mother, no great fan of Ethel, had repeatedly warned her daughter about 'that wicked English girl'. Eventually, she told Lisl that she must choose between Ethel or her family – no idle threat since, as Ethel realized, 'In Austria, the family is sacrosanct.'[14]

However, before this ultimatum was issued, events took a surprising turn. In 1882, on a visit to Florence, Ethel was introduced to Lisl's sister, Julia, and Julia's husband, Henry ('HB') Brewster, a writer and poet. It appears that, initially, it was Julia Brewster who interested her: 'I am carefully preventing myself from getting fond of her, as I don't think she would know what to do with my affection,' she wrote.[15] What she could not prevent, however, was Harry Brewster falling head over heels in love with her. He told Julia immediately and, according to Ethel, 'with her approval went off to Africa to shoot lions and get over his infatuation'.[16] We have no record of how many unfortunate lions were sacrificed in the name of his love, but it certainly did no good. To make matters worse, two years later, Ethel claimed to reciprocate his feelings. For the next ten years or so, this odd couple upset everybody with their on-off, intense romantic friendship. During this time, Julia Brewster fought vainly to prevent HB and Ethel seeing each other, while Lisl was distraught at Ethel's latest emotional shenanigans. But Ethel did not want to let her go: as late as 1890, she was still hoping 'that the day of reconciliation with his sister-in-law, Lisl, might yet dawn; Lisl, the matchless musician whom I loved more than anyone in the world, whose charm, beauty and tenderness sometimes haunt me even now in dreams. ...'[17]

It was not to be: Lisl died in 1892, the rift between her and Ethel never healed. This was largely due, as far as Ethel was concerned, to Julia who had apparently 'let Lisl die without permitting her to send me one loving word'. Her response was bitter: 'I should henceforth shape my life as though she, Julia, did not exist.'[18] It is no coincidence that, at this point, she decided that her relationship with Harry Brewster should be physically consummated – the ultimate revenge against Julia.

Such was the bitterness between them that, when Julia herself died in 1896, a rumour spread that Ethel had had a hand in her death. Despite this, Harry Brewster discussed the possibility of marriage with Ethel but, not unsurprisingly, she was against the idea and the very suggestion seemed to alter their relationship. 'In our case the result was that I found myself gradually beginning to hate HB,'[19] she recalled.

There is no doubt that HB had a huge influence on her work

and thoughts – she was always quoting him to friends before and after his death from cancer in 1908. But she was as merciless with him at the height of their affair as she was with her women: she would make fun of his beard and his clothes, and would have no compunction in summoning him to meet her at short notice at rendezvous up and down the country. In a letter to him in 1892, she wrote:

> I wonder why it is so much easier for me to love my own sex passionately rather than yours? Even my love for my mother had an intense quality you can only call passion. How do you account for it? I am a very healthy minded person and it is an everlasting puzzle.[20]

He replied, 'these affections entail no duties, no sacrifice of liberty or of tastes, no partial loss of individuality'.[21] But she was always quick to defend her 'puzzling' passionate attachments to women: she told the disgruntled HB, 'What surprises me is that everyone is not in the same boat.'[22] But the writer Vernon Lee (Violet Paget) challenged her on this: 'To how many people have you given without reserve and got something like the equivalent in return?' Ethel replied that there were three: Lisl, Harry and a third, unnamed, person. Lee deduced that she was probably referring to Lady Ponsonby, one of Queen Victoria's ladies-in-waiting who, Ethel said, satisfied 'that yearning for motherly affection'.[23]

Although the Lisl–Julia–Harry merry-go-round dominated her life during these years, there were plenty of diversions. In the early 1890s, she met the Benson family. When E. F. Benson's first novel, *Dodo*, was published in 1893, Ethel was immortalized as the central character's 'candid friend', Edith Staines, a young lady who ate eggs and bacon on the lid of her piano while composing. With or without the benefit of bacon and eggs, Ethel was busy: among the works composed in this period were *Fantasio*, a comic opera (1892–4); the Mass in D (inspired by her love for the Catholic, Pauline Trevelyan); and Serenade in D, which was her first work to be performed in England, at Crystal Palace in 1890.

In 1894, her father died and Frimhurst was left to her brother, Bob. Ethel was left a paltry £300 'to buy furniture'. She did so, and moved the items into her new home, a rented cottage nearby which she dubbed 'One Oak'. During her years here, she employed a female servant, Ford, who was something of a colourful character. One day Ethel's GP, a Dr Vandrey, informed her that Ford had struck up a liaison with an officer of his acquaintance stationed at Aldershot. This soldier, on learning that Ethel was one of the doctor's patients, asked what she was like. 'Quite mad', replied Dr Vandrey. Some weeks later, the soldier informed the incredulous doctor that he and Ethel were 'now on kissing terms'. Dr Vandrey asked what his kissing partner looked like and soon realized what had happened. The soldier was not amused to be told that he had, in fact, been canoodling with Ford. When Dr Vandrey told Ethel the whole story, he explained how he knew from the start that she had not been locked in passionate embraces with the officer: 'I didn't think that your madness takes that particular form.'[24]

One of her Hampshire neighbours happened to be the Empress Eugénie, the exiled widow of Napoleon III. Ethel 'saw her constantly, travelled with her, stayed in her houses, lived practically next door to her for more than thirty years and who eagerly sought her company'.[25] It was an unlikely friendship: Eugénie had no empathy with Ethel's two main passions – music and women. Ethel once said of her, 'Anyone more totally devoid of musical instinct I have seldom met'[26] and, one day, when they were discussing what they called 'Sapphism', Eugénie confessed, 'I don't understand – I don't know what they do!' Ethel wryly noted, 'to elderly people like her whose whole sexual endowment was probably sparse to start with, a good many things must remain a mystery'.[27]

However, it was this unlikely confidante and supporter who was to be instrumental in promoting Ethel's music. Ethel was under no illusions about the role played by her connections: 'Let it be pointed out that very few girls happen to live next door to rich Empresses of pronounced feministic sympathies'.[28] Eugénie gave her financial support and brought her to the attention of the Duke of Edinburgh, the President of the Royal Choral Society.

The Mass in D was performed at the Royal Albert Hall in 1893. Ethel's verdict: 'Reception: Enthusiastic. Press: Devastating.'[29] This was a slight exaggeration: J. A. Fuller-Maitland, music critic of the London *Times* wrote, 'This work definitely places the composer amongst the most eminent composers of her time, and easily at the head of all those of her sex.' George Bernard Shaw predicted, 'It is interesting as the beginning of what I have so often prophesied – the conquest of popular music by women.'[30] But the Mass was not performed again until 1924. From 1893 to 1933, there were only nineteen performances in England of Ethel Smyth's major choral works – mainly the Mass – and only one recording – *The Wreckers* overture, on Columbia. Ethel was in a Catch-22 situation, which she recognized: 'Unperformed music cannot hope for records.'[31] In contrast, there were regular performances of her works in several European countries.

In the meantime, she continued to compose, albeit erratically. *The Prison* was based on Harry Brewster's metaphysical poem of the same name; *Fête Galante* on a short story by another close friend, the novelist Maurice Baring. HB also wrote the libretto for Ethel's best-known opera *The Wreckers* (1904). Originally written in French, it was inspired by a holiday in Cornwall, where she had visited smugglers' caves. The opera, *A Cornish Drama in 3 Acts*, was set in the mid-eighteenth century, during the early days of the Wesleyan revival, in a community which believed that shipwrecking was not only right but would bring divine favour upon them.

Ethel maintained that she composed for the 'general music-loving public'. In the programme notes for concerts of her music, she wrote, 'Listeners are specially invited to applaud *whenever they feel like it* – ES.'[32] The explanation she gave for her erratic musical output was that 'Attention to business was sometimes interrupted by an inordinate flow of passion in three directions – sport, games and friendship.'[33] It was also diverted in another direction: the path towards women's suffrage. She was introduced to Emmeline Pankhurst in 1910 and promptly decided to devote the next two years of her life to the Women's Social and Political Union. Although never straying from her customary attire of tweed suits, she always tried to wear an item of clothing that bore the WPSU colours of white, green and purple.

Ethel's involvement was immortalized in the television series *Shoulder to Shoulder*. In one scene, Lady Plessey introduces her to

Emmeline Pankhurst; she immediately pledges her allegiance to the cause and promises to write the suffragettes a theme tune: 'Every great cause needs a tune – a thumping great march!' Off she strides across the lawn, leaving Mrs Pankhurst musing, 'I rather liked her'.

She is next seen conducting her *March of the Women* – with lyrics by Cicely Hamilton – on Coronation Day, which the suffragettes had designated 'Suffrage Day'. Next, prior to a window-smashing campaign, she gives stone-throwing lessons to Emmeline, who manages to hurl a rock *backwards*, straight onto the head of Ethel's dog, Pan. Ethel's eventual target was the home of a cabinet minister, 'Lulu' Harcourt, the Colonial Secretary. She was imprisoned for two months and put in a cell next to Mrs Pankhurst. After their arrest, a new influx of women prisoners troop to their cells singing *March* as Ethel conducts them through the cell bars with her toothbrush. Of her time in Holloway, she commented, 'The ravages of prison fare on delicate digestions could hardly be exaggerated!'[34] However, she also observed, 'I have often reflected that during those two months in Holloway for the first and last time of my life I was in good society. Think of it! more than 100 women together ... forgetful of everything save the idea for which they had faced imprisonment.'[35]

Apart from her devotion to 'the cause', Ethel had, of course, fallen deeply in love with Emmeline Pankhurst. And though the eminent feminist was far from being a lifelong lesbian, she did not appear to spurn Ethel's advances. Ethel was rapturous. 'I think it is the crowning achievement of my life to have made you love me,' she told her 'darling Em'.[36] Later, when Ethel had moved to Surrey, Emmeline Pankhurst, in poor health and tired of the eternal police presence outside her London home, often stayed with her to recuperate. The police merely followed her to Surrey. Appropriately, when a statue of Mrs Pankhurst was unveiled outside the House of Commons in 1930, it was Ethel who conducted the Metropolitan Police Band (ironically enough) in the *March of the Women* and the chorale from *The Wreckers*.

Having completed her allotted two years as a suffragette, she travelled to Egypt, where she wrote the opera, *The Boatswain's Mate*. She then visited Vienna, Munich and Brittany. By 1914, she had managed to negotiate contracts for it to be performed at the

Frankfurt Opera House and *The Wreckers* at the Munich Opera House in February 1915. She was celebrating her achievements in Brittany when a fatal shot was fired in Sarajevo and the First World War erupted.

She stayed in France throughout the war and trained as a radiographer. She became a voluntary 'localizer' attached to the Thirteenth Division of the French army in Vichy Hospital. She also found time to pen her two-volume memoir, *Impressions That Remained*, published to great acclaim in 1919. Unintentionally, she had embarked on a literary career, producing volumes of autobiography and travel books, for which she would become more famous than her music.

When the war ended, and after a bout of pleurisy and pneumonia, she visited Sicily with her latest 'passion', Edith Somerville, one half of the Somerville and Ross writing team. Ethel noted that Edith's sister, Nina (Mrs Herbert Hollings), had also found 'a new *culte*, Gleichen's youngest sister, Helena. Even before HH's death they were inseparable; after it they set up home together and have lived together ever since'.[37] Helena Gleichen was an artist; during the war, she and Nina were part of a mobile ambulance unit and were eventually decorated for valour in Italy.

After more excursions abroad, Ethel settled in to a new home, Coign, at Hook Heath near Woking. In 1922, she was made a Dame Commander of the Order of the British Empire. She continued to pour out her memoirs with admirable regularity: *Streaks of Life* (1921); *Female Pipings in Eden* (1933); *As Time Went On* (1936); and *What Happened Next* (1940). In many of them, she continued to reproach the patriarchal British musical establishment, not only for its failure to encourage women musicians and composers but also for its outdated attitudes towards opera. She declared:

> Goodbye to the illusion that opera is a living issue in England. So it will remain till we class opera with public pleasure grounds as a luxury that a civilised community demands, that cannot pay its way and must be subsidised.[38]

The alternative, she said, was for British composers to try their luck abroad, but doubted that many had either the time or the money to do so.

She berated the Hallé Orchestra in Manchester for sacking all its women musicians on the grounds that, when touring, they had trouble finding accommodation for them; and that it was also in 'the interests of "Unity of Style" '.[39] She sounded out in similar fashion when the BBC Orchestra banned women cellists from its ranks: 'Perhaps the attitude of the cello player is considered an unseemly one for women? If not propriety, the idea can only be to keep women in their place.'[40] She encouraged other women to take action against the invisibility of female musicians and composers:

> Form yourselves into a sort of 'Society for the Prevention of Cruelty to Women Musicians' and swear that unless women are given equal chances with men in the orchestra and unless women's work figures in your programmes, *you will make things very disagreeable all round.*[41]

Although she still found the musical establishment indifferent to her talents, she was, almost until her dying day, able to satisfy her enormous appetite for friendships. During one of her holidays in Italy, she had met the writer Vernon Lee, then ensconced in a villa near Florence. Lee declared that 'Miss Smyth's singing is not music – it is combustible literature'[42] – as fine an example of a backhanded compliment as you could wish for. Lee employed an Italian cook who would serve up a curious array of stomach-churning dishes: house specialities included tongue stewed in chocolate and bird's claw omelettes.

Ethel also became friends with 'The Boys' of Smallhythe. She met them in 1911 during a trip to see Edy Craig about Vernon Lee's play, *Ariadne*. Ethel and Christopher St John fell out over Catholicism: 'Catholics are a feeble lot, especially if they are converts,' Ethel sneered. During her infatuation with Pauline Trevelyan, she herself had once been tempted to convert, but told Chris that when she wrote her Mass 'I think that sweated it out of me. ....'[43]

When the Mass in D enjoyed a rare performance in

Birmingham in February 1924, Chris wrote a review of it in *Time and Tide*. She enthused, 'there hasn't been such a sensation since Mendelssohn dug out the St Matthew Passion after a hundred years' neglect'.[44] A few years before her death, Ethel asked Chris to be her literary executor. Chris was under no illusions: 'I was no more than an understudy of much closer friends'[45] – most of whom were, by then, dead.

When she was in her seventies, she began the friendship she described as 'the greatest joy of my latter end'.[46] She met Virginia Woolf in February 1930 and was instantly smitten; Woolf's nephew and biographer, Quentin Bell, believed that she was in love with his aunt before she had even met her. Initially, however, Virginia recoiled: 'An old woman of seventy-one has fallen in love with me,' she wrote. 'It is at once hideous and horrid and melancholy-sad. It is like being caught by a crab.'[47] But the 'crab' was not insensitive to the limitations of any relationship with the troubled writer: 'One can't have relations with her as with others. The fact is you have to take what you can get of Virginia,' she reasoned.[48]

This did not stop her badgering Virginia when her letters were not answered promptly and enthusiastically, or of being jealous of Virginia's other female intimates. She confessed, 'I have never loved anyone so much ... I had not meant to tell you. But I want affection. You may take advantage of this.'[49] Ethel got the affection she was seeking but not, as she may have hoped, to the exclusion of all others. Virginia told Ethel she only loved three people: her husband Leonard, her sister Vanessa Bell and Vita Sackville-West. Vita told her husband, Harold Nicolson, that this rather annoyed Ethel. She was close to Vanessa but her relations with Leonard Woolf were less than cordial.

Inevitably, these two grand eccentrics were always falling out: Virginia found Ethel too demanding, and Ethel disapproved of many members of the Bloomsbury circle. They seemed to average one major row a year, usually ending with Virginia vowing never to see her again – but something always brought them back together. Whatever it was, Virginia made it clear it was certainly not Ethel's table manners, an issue on which she was particularly sensitive. Virginia, it seems, did not appreciate Ethel blowing her nose on her napkin or pouring cream meant for blackberries into her beer. Vita

Sackville-West met her for lunch in May 1938 and recalled that it was not a great success: Ethel's hair was a mess and she kept blowing her nose on her scarf.

In 1934, in celebration of her seventy-fifth birthday, a number of concerts were held in her honour and *The Wreckers* was revived at Sadler's Wells. Sadly, she was able to hear very little, as she had become increasingly deaf during the previous twenty years. Vita Sackville-West described her cumbersome hearing trumpet as looking 'like a cinema apparatus' which Ethel managed to use the wrong way round. This robust woman, for so many years able to indulge her enthusiasm for tennis, golf and mountaineering, was finally succumbing to the limitations imposed by the ageing process. This was brought home once and for all in a humiliating episode. One night, in February 1942, she had to use a chamber-pot, which broke underneath her. Ethel lay on the floor all night, wet and cold. She suffered concussion and spent several weeks recovering in a nursing home. Ethel recovered but from then on had a constant nurse/companion, a Miss Brook, and was never quite the same again. However, she insisted on getting up and dressed each day, declaring, 'I intend to die standing up.'[50] By 1943, she was completely deaf and conversations could only be held by writing notes. Chris St John noticed that Nurse Brook insisted on dressing her charge in 'most unbecoming lady-like clothes'.[51] But, as Kathleen Dale, her musical executor said, 'There was nothing in her appearance to suggest a delicate old lady and nothing in her manner to inspire pity.'[52]

She did not, as she wished, die standing up, but was carried off by a bout of pneumonia on 8 May 1944, aged eighty-six. She was cremated and her ashes were scattered in the woods adjacent to Woking Golf Course. Kathleen Dale declared, 'With Ethel Smyth's death the musical world lost a picturesque personality who can never be replaced' and 'Ethel Smyth holds a unique position in the annals of musical history as a composer who won equal fame as a writer.'[53] Vita Sackville-West wrote a poem to Ethel, celebrating her as a 'wild welcomer of life, of love, of art'.[54] Christopher St John, meanwhile, went to Coign to begin cataloguing all Ethel's papers, letters, cuttings and manuscripts. It took nearly two years.

After her death, there was no notable increase in the performances or recordings of her work. It was primarily her books, plus St John's excellent 1959 biography, which kept her name in the public consciousness. But she was immortalized in other forms. Ethel was one of the thirty-nine women celebrated in Judy Chicago's 'Last Supper' installation, *The Dinner Party*, an enormous triangular table set with special, vagina-shaped 'plates' commemorating thirty-nine women, with another 999 names in the floor tiles. It was first seen in San Francisco in 1979, and was eventually brought to England in 1985. Ethel's plate showed an open grand piano balanced on a flattened man's jacket.

But, at the time of writing, as the fiftieth anniversary of her death drew closer, her music was being rediscovered and celebrated. In 1991, a CD was released, containing her Mass in D, the *March of the Women* and nine minutes of *The Boatswain's Mate*. Her Trio in D minor for violin, cello and piano, written in 1880, was given its first performance in England at the Purcell Room in London in May 1993. A month before, at the Royal Festival Hall, the European Women's Orchestra, conducted by Odaline de la Martinez, performed a programme of her music before a rapturous, virtually all-women audience. Martinez told the *Independent on Sunday*: 'Her work has to be performed with a real sense of style. Her music has to be played larger than life. If we play it in a measured, held-back way, it doesn't work.'[55] And that, essentially, was the key to her music: it was an extension of her character and her passions. As Vita Sackville-West said, 'her letters and books are all the same – they are HER'.[56]

Perhaps this larger-than-life woman can be best summed up in the crude but effective tribute paid to her in *The Gay Book of Days*: 'Ethel Smyth had balls.'

Notes

1. Ronald Crichton, *The Memoirs of Ethel Smyth* (abridged) (London, Viking, 1987), p. 23.
2. *Ibid.*, p. 25.
3. *Ibid.*
4. *Ibid.*, p. 27.
5. *Ibid.*, p. 44.
6. *Ibid.*, p. 53.

7. Christopher St John, *Ethel Smyth: A Biography* (London, Longmans, 1959), p. 43.
8. Ethel Smyth, *As Time Went On* (London, Longmans, 1936), p. 10.
9. *Ibid.*, p. 218.
10. *Ibid.*
11. Crichton, *Memoirs*, p. 96.
12. Ethel Smyth, *Impressions That Remained*, 2 vols. (London, Longmans, 1919), pp. 192–3.
13. Crichton, *Memoirs*, p. 132.
14. Smyth, *As Time*, pp. 9–10.
15. St John, *Ethel Smyth*, p. 43.
16. Smyth, *As Time*, p. 7.
17. Ethel Smyth, *What Happened Next* (London, Longmans, 1940), p. 3.
18. *Ibid.*, p. 13.
19. *Ibid.*, p. 22.
20. Smyth, *As Time*, p. 156.
21. *Ibid.*, p. 159.
22. St John, *Ethel Smyth*, p. 117.
23. *Ibid.*, p. 76.
24. Ethel Smyth, *Streaks of Life* (London, Longmans, 1921), p. 77.
25. *Ibid.*, p. 5.
26. *Ibid.*, p. 23.
27. Smyth, *As Time*, p. 214.
28. Ethel Smyth, *Female Pipings in Eden* (London, Peter Davies, 1933), p. 39.
29. *Ibid.*
30. *Ibid.*, p. 295.
31. *Ibid.*, p. 296.
32. St John, *Ethel Smyth*, p. 304.
33. Crichton, *Memoirs*, p. 360.
34. Smyth, *Pipings in Eden*, p. 210.
35. *Ibid.*, p. 211.
36. Piers Brendon, *Eminent Edwardians* (London, Book Club Associates, 1979), p. 175.
37. Smyth, *What Happened*, p. 259.
38. Smyth, *Streaks*, p. 219.
39. *Ibid.*, p. 240.
40. Smyth, *Pipings in Eden*, p. 11.
41. *Ibid.*, p. 51.
42. Smyth, *What Happened*, p. 27.
43. St John, *Ethel Smyth*, p. xvi.
44. *Ibid.*, p. 184.
45. *Ibid.*, p. xvii.

46.   *Ibid.*, p. 237.
47.   Quentin Bell, *Virginia Woolf* (London, Hogarth Press, 1972), p. 151.
48.   St John, *Ethel Smyth*, p. 222.
49.   Bell, *Virginia Woolf*, p. 154.
50.   St John, *Ethel Smyth*, p. 242.
51.   *Ibid.*
52.   *Ibid.*, p. 258.
53.   *Ibid.*, pp. 304 and 288.
54.   *Ibid.*, p. xiii.
55.   *Independent on Sunday*, 11 April 1993.
56.   St John, *Ethel Smyth*, p. 246.

Eve Balfour: 'The Compost Queen'

THERE is an old Scottish family – the Balfours – whose coat of arms bears the motto, 'Virtus ad aethera tendit' ('Virtue strives towards heaven'). This lofty, rather puritanical declaration was clearly taken to heart by several of the first Earl's descendants. His sons threw themselves into public and political life and, except for one, raised large, close-knit families – the epitome of so-called 'Victorian values'. The son who remained resolutely unmarried was nevertheless devoted to the other members of his sprawling clan and outdid his brothers by becoming Prime Minister, striving towards heaven in his own way as the most well-known Balfour of them all. But, although it is the name of Arthur Balfour which figures largest in the history books and encyclopaedias, it is actually one of his nieces whose influence remains strong today.

It is a common misconception that concern for the environment, the questioning of conventional, mass-farming methods and the increasing trend towards the production and consumption of organic produce are issues that only came into public consciousness in the 1980s. From the comfortable bosom of the aristocratic Balfour family came a woman with a strong claim to the title of 'Mother Earth'. For although Eve Balfour was not the only founder of the modern organic farming movement, it was her efforts which kept its torch glowing with over fifty years of dedicated research and campaigning.

Lady Evelyn Barbara Balfour was born in July 1898. Her father, Gerald, second Earl of Balfour, was primarily involved in politics – he served as Chief Secretary for Ireland and was President of the Board of Trade – but also devoted a good part of his life to studying psychic phenomena. In 1887, he married Lady Elizabeth Bulwer-Lytton, daughter of Lord Lytton, poet and Viceroy of India. They had a son and five daughters: Robert, Nell, Ruth, Mary, Evelyn and Kathleen. One of Eve's aunts was the first principal of Newnham College, Cambridge. But her most famous relative was her uncle, the philosopher and eventual Conservative Prime Minister, Arthur Balfour, known to the younger members of the family as 'Nunkie'.

For much of Eve's childhood, six months of every year were spent at the Balfour ancestral home of Whittingehame in Scotland, along with numerous members of the clan. Another uncle, Eustace, brought his wife and five children and the two families lived virtually as one. 'Nunkie', being the eldest of the Balfour brothers, had inherited Whittingehame but was, as they say, unmarried and so almost regarded his many nephews and nieces as his own. Eve was particularly fond of her sisters, Ruth and Nell, and their cousins, Joan and Alison, a close-knit group known throughout the family as 'Us-Four'. Eve later said that they, together with 'Nunkie', were the people who (apart from her parents) were the most influential in her education and upbringing. She described her days at Whittingehame as 'a wonderful carefree existence', although with so many siblings, literal or otherwise, there was an element of 'survival of the fittest'.

But it was 'Nunkie' who remained the most important person in the children's lives. 'Like the different spokes of a wheel, our lives revolved round the same hub – AJ', Eve explained. '[He] managed to be both an oracle and a contemporary to his horde of nieces'.[1] Although 'Us-Four' monopolized 'Nunkie', the younger members of the extended Balfour family were not neglected. Their kindly uncle provided ponies for them and regular trips were taken to the nearby seaside, six miles away, or up into the hills of Lammermuir – seventh heaven for the horse- and swimming-mad Eve.

At Christmas and New Year, more strands of the clan would assemble for the festivities, presided over by 'Nunkie' and Eve's father. 'Then all the old family jokes were retailed again, and new ones added. Family talk leapt from the profound to the ridiculous,' recalled Eve.[2] Another of Eve's notable cousins present at the annual knees-up would be the composer Elizabeth Lutyens. Their aunt, the suffragette Lady Constance Lytton described the young Lutyens as having 'something of the peculiar character-charm of Eve only more charm in the outer-coating, more tenderness and dumpy womanliness, less tomboy than Eve'.[3]

Eve decided she wanted to be a vegetarian at the age of seven when, during a shooting party, a pheasant fell dead at her feet. Five years later, in a similarly swift decision, she told her parents she wanted to become a farmer. They had no objections and agreed that she would enrol as a student on the agricultural course at University College, Reading. She began her studies when she was seventeen and earned a Diploma in Agriculture.

No sooner had she qualified than she found herself, at twenty, training and supervising Land Army girls on a farm during the First World War, which she later described as, 'Quite an adventure – they were all older than me and they were tough.' She would never have been put in charge if she had not lied about her age, saying she was several years older.

In 1917, with most of the rural labour force fighting in the trenches rather than digging in fields, the Women's Land Army was formed to counter the threat of food shortages. The Ministry of Agriculture created a branch within its walls with the specific brief of supplying women workers to farms. It was staffed entirely by women.

Initially, the scheme faced several major problems: many women who would have come forward for such work had already joined the WRNS and the WAAF and other sections of the armed forces. Secondly, the farmers themselves were sceptical about using women workers, particularly since there was little time available for training – at one point during the war, there was only enough food left to feed the nation for three weeks. Then there were other more basic problems, such as suitable accommodation, working conditions and wages. But after these were solved, the WLA was quickly mobilized. It even had its own magazine, *The Landswoman*. Forty-five thousand women applied but only 23,000 were accepted for work. They worked as milkers, tractor-drivers, field workers, carters, thatchers and shepherds. Lord Ernle, the Agriculture Minister in 1918, declared, 'In all of them, women have excelled.'[4] Each county had a Women's Agricultural Committee; travelling inspectors supervised the work and each village had a group leader. The WLA was disbanded in 1919 but re-formed again in the autumn of 1938, almost immediately after Neville Chamberlain had waved his paper from Hitler and promised 'Peace in our Time'.

In 1919, Eve and her sister Mary, who had also trained to be a farmer, fulfilled their childhood ambition and rented New Bells Farm in Haughley, Suffolk, featuring a moated farmhouse dating back to 1450 and a thousand-year-old oak tree. The farm was not cheap: £25 an acre for 156 acres. Beryl 'Beb' Hearnden joined them as a working partner. She once declared that 'the world seemed to be divided into men, women and Theosophists'.[5] We assume she considered herself to be one of the latter.

Elizabeth Lutyens was a regular visitor to the farm during her teens, spending many weekends and holidays there. On her first visit, she was presented with a simple but strange meal: Welsh rarebit and *stewed* lettuce. Her description of life at New Bells conjures up a vivid picture, both of the farm and of her country cousin:

> I loved the life there, free and unconventional and dominated by the warm strength of Eve's personality. She had an Egyptian face of great strength and charm, with cropped hair and masculine manners, in spite of a feminine heart. She would stride about the farm pipe in mouth and in trousers. ... Farm girls and other friends lived around in pretty cottages, all gathering in the big main dining room for meals.[6]

Lutyens loved the atmosphere at Haughley: it freed her from the 'goldfish bowl of the musical world of which I was gradually becoming a part', and also prevented her family pressurizing her into leading the life of a debutante. Eventually, she built a timber cottage-cum-barn in one of the fields at Haughley, dubbed 'Braughlies', as her very own country bolt-hole.

After a hard day's toil in the fields, the New Bells gels would get out their instruments: Eve played saxophone, Mary the ukelele and Beb the piano. They played *le jazz hot*. Or, at least, tepid: Beb once orchestrated a Brahms song for the band to perform – not perhaps the best choice for the instruments at her disposal. Eventually, they were invited to play at friends' parties and this in turn led to a regular gig on Saturday nights at the Great White Horse Inn in Ipswich, called 'The Pickwick Dance Club'. Apart from anything else, they needed the money. According to Mary Langman, of the Wholefood Trust, 'They were farming seriously, but undercapitalised and relatively inexperienced, in the great agricultural depression between the wars, when established farmers all round them were going bankrupt. So a little cash from peripheral activities came in very useful.'[7]

Money was also the prime motivation for Eve and Beb's excursions into the field of pot-boiler crime novels. Under the pseudonym of 'Hearnden Balfour', they co-wrote three detective novels, which seemed to draw on Eve's aristocratic and political background. The first, *The Paper Chase*, published in 1927, was the tale of amateur sleuth, Jim Crawley, in love with Judy, daughter of crooked Lord Fairleigh, owner of Coombe Castle in Devon. Enter Crawley's boss, American millionaire, Bill Boyd. Boyd wants to get better acquainted with Fairleigh and, when it transpires that the American is the true heir to the Fairleigh title, the naughty noble locks him in the castle dungeons, leaving Crawley and his friends to solve the mystery. The *Times Literary Supplement* commented that 'Mr Balfour [*sic*] ... has provided all the ingredients – secret passages and even a ghost – of an exciting story'.

The next offering, *The Enterprising Burglar* (1928) , which was dedicated to 'All the shareholders in New Bells, Unlimited', could not have been more different from the first. It was essentially the story of one Stephen 'Nick' Nicholson, an ex-soldier-cum-'Robin Hood' burglar, who lived a dual life as an East End navvy, on close terms with a Scotland Yard detective. But the core of the plot involved his hunt for the head of a revolutionary organization with firm footholds in every major industrial centre in Britain. Enterprising indeed.

The last novel, *Anything Might Happen*, was published in 1931. This time, the central figure was a woman, Kit Dundas, secretary in a firm of London lawyers. Kit's work sometimes takes her abroad and, returning to England from one of these trips, she meets a young man on the boat, Mark Treganza, who is sub-sequently arrested at Dover. As you might have guessed, Kit turns detective and becomes embroiled in a less than thrilling plot involv-ing a murderer, an innocent man, dope smuggling and a mysterious figure known to the police as 'VLS'.

Eve sent copies of the books to 'Nunkie'. Other members of her family had been scathing about her literary attempts but her uncle declared, 'I note with pleasure the steady improvement which marks the character of the family literature. It has now blossomed into the only kind of writing really worth bothering about − that, namely, which gives much pleasure, and no instruction!'[8]

During the 1930s, Eve, her partners and their farming neigh-bours were involved in a long-drawn-out battle, dating back to the Middle Ages, which itself had all the ingredients of a thriller: police, lawyers, rural rebellion and cow-napping.

The centuries-old tithe laws decreed that a tenth of the annual produce of the farms be levied for support of the clergy, the upkeep of church buildings and poor relief. Over the years, the poor saw far less of this money than the Church, and farmers had rebelled against the rate of tithes in countries throughout England, Ireland and Wales. In the 1930s, it was the turn of those in East Anglia.

Despite her background, Eve and her partners were no better positioned to pay the tithes than their neighbours who, like them, were still struggling to remain solvent after the farming de-pression. Determined to bring about the end of an unjust law, the Suffolk farmers united to thwart the enforcement of tithe collec-tions or 'distraints'.

Under the existing law, livestock could be seized by bailiffs in lieu of tithe arrears. However, these seizures were only legal if they were carried out between sunset and sunrise and only if the animals were not locked in a barn or shed. It was imperative, therefore, for the rebelling farmers to be vigilant so that their herds could be safely locked up before the bailiffs and police set foot on their land. Consequently, these attempts would often lead to head-on confrontations.

In May 1933, a group of farmers descended on Delvyn's

Farm to stop bailiffs seizing livestock in respect of £48 in unpaid tithes owed by Margaret Pickett Gardiner. The bailiffs and their solicitor met with a somewhat hostile reception, during which eggs and wheat-chaff were thrown at them and, ultimately, they were 'jostled and imprisoned in a barn'.[9]

On 7 July, bailiffs arrived at New Bells Farm where, as reported in *The Times*, 'In spite of some resistance by men on the farm, a number of dairy cows were loaded onto lorries'.[10] Members of the Suffolk Tithepayers' Association arrived at the farm only minutes after the cows had been spirited away. But Eve remained resolute: she told a meeting of the Association that she would not stop the protests against these tithe distraints until the law was altered.

The next month, Eve and thirty-six other farmers were summoned before Castle Hedingham magistrates to face a charge that 'You did (on May 23 1933) unlawfully assemble together against the peace of our Sovereign Lord the King, his crown and dignity'.[11] At the subsequent trial at Essex Assizes in Chelmsford, all defendants pleaded not guilty. During the proceedings, evidence given by one bailiff about the fracas is hilarious in its understatement: 'There was a little bit of bad language between one or two of the people', and the lawyer, George Gibson, received 'a rotten egg in the back of the neck'. Things began to look even more perilous for this hapless pair when, apparently, they were threatened with a hive of bees. After one day, the judge decided there was no evidence against five of the defendants.

As for Eve's involvement, the court heard she was 'standing on a straw-baler'. Was there any riotous conduct on her part, asked defending counsel, Melford Stevenson. Apparently not. Was she, in fact, telling the crowd to let the solicitor and bailiff out of the barn and urging them not to resist the police? 'Something to that effect,' said the witness. The accused herself took the witness stand on 3 November. She told the court that she knew about the impending raid on Delvyn's Farm and had asked to be informed when the bailiffs arrived, as she wished to amass evidence about the firm responsible for the tithe collections. She only entered the barn in question, she said, to eat some bread and cheese and that she did not see the offending eggs and chaff being thrown. Needless to say, it was not too long before the prosecution case against her crumbled.

Her battles did not go unnoticed: in one of her numerous volumes of memoirs, Ethel Smyth noted:

> At this very moment a fuss is going on in East Anglia about unjust tithes, and lo! two women farmers, nieces of one of our great politicians – a half-friend of the type Mrs Pankhurst hated and despised more than an enemy – have been heading a rebellion, rescuing a cow that was about to be distrained and routing the police! I think if those two ringleaders had listened carefully they might have heard a voice whispering in their ear: 'Well done, women!'[12]

Although she was something of a reluctant radical, Eve's campaign against the tithe continued. In April 1934, while the government's new Tithe Bill was being considered by the House of Lords, she wrote a letter to *The Times*, warning of the legislation's pitfalls and its possible effects on both workers and land:

> It benefits the tithe owner and makes the lot of the farmer worse. ... Unless it is thrown out or drastically revised the next page in the history of agriculture will be the blackest ever. The new Bill turns tithe into a land tax ... Tithe up to two-fifths of the annual rent-value of the land will have to be paid whether there is any income to pay it with or not ... The harassed farmer will have to sell stock or sack labour ... We shall soon see our gaols full of hard-working but un-protected agricultural labourers. In the meantime, what is to happen to the land?[13]

The government set up a Royal Commission to sort out the tithe question and Eve was among those to give evidence. Again, she emphasized the social effects of excessive tithes: 'The danger of growing bitterness cannot be exaggerated and I appeal most strongly that the Commission should realize it before all faith in the Church and in English justice is lost to the farming population.' She pleaded for the abolition of all tithes, on the grounds that

I think it might save the Church from being utterly discredited. There are quite a lot of us who would prefer to regard the Church as a spiritual force in the land, and not as a financial corporation concerned only with its dividends.

She also took the opportunity to complain about the irregularity of collection methods and the partiality of the police which, together, led to cases of 'pure victimization'. She told how she had seen 'the destruction of property, wanton and sickening cruelty to animals and assault carried out under police protection'.[14] Not bad for a reluctant radical.

Eve's first twenty years of farming followed conventional methods of husbandry. But in 1938, she read Lord Lymington's *Famine in England*, which questioned orthodox farming methods. He believed that, far from bringing an abundance of food, such methods would eventually have the opposite effect. Eve decided to test his theories by carrying out practical scientific research into the effects of soil treatment on plants, animals and humans. To this end, the Balfours pooled resources and land with their neighbour, Alice Debenham of Walnut Tree Farm, and established the 200-acre Haughley Experiment, dedicated solely to organic farming research.

The experiment started in 1939, when the farm was divided into three units. One was set aside purely for arable farming; the other two were, alternately, used for temporary pasture and arable farming. On each of them lived a herd of dairy cows, poultry and a small flock of sheep. All the animals were fed exclusively on the food grown on their unit. Only surplus animals were sold. On one of these two identical units, called 'The Mixed Section', a selection of chemical fertilizers, insecticides and fungicides was used, while on the other one, 'The Organic Section', no chemicals of any sort were applied.

Within a few years, the Haughley Experiment yielded some interesting results: the animals living off the organic section were more contented and seemed to have longer lives. Animal products, such as meat, milk and eggs, required nearly 15 per cent less food when it was organic. Over a twenty-year period, the cows fed organically produced 25 per cent more milk than their chemically reared counterparts.

After Eve's death, Dr Victor Stewart, a soil scientist and consultant, described Haughley as a project 'the like of which our Universities and Ministries are never likely to emulate even in the wake of the current scramble to benefit from the organic bandwagon'. It was ignored by government and the agricultural scientific establishment because, he asserted, they 'were naively self-confident of their ability to dominate Nature. They had no interest in ecological constraints that might limit production'.[15] And it was ever thus, despite a few token gestures: in December 1969, the Minister of Agriculture ordered an 'urgent' investigation to establish whether or not 'modern farming practices are damaging soil fertility and structure'; and 1970 was declared 'International Conservation Year'.

In 1943, Eve published her book, *The Living Soil*, with the intention of garnering support for the research being carried out at Haughley. It was written in the wake of another farming depression and, in between working on it in the evenings and her usual tasks at New Bells, she also served as an air-raid warden. At this time, she was paying herself no more than the average farm worker's wages.

The Living Soil outlined her theories on sustainable farming and alternative approaches to the food chain. Her views remain as relevant today as then. The fundamental theme was the relationship between the health of soil, plants, animals and human beings. She wrote:

> Health is not a state, but a living process consisting of a mutual synthesis between organism and environment. My subject is food, which concerns everyone; it is health, which concerns everyone; it is the soil which concerns everyone – though they may not realise it – and it is the history of certain recent researches linking these three vital subjects.[16]

She asserted that the nutritional value of food was profoundly affected by conditions of growth and treatment, and that the activities of the flora and fauna in soil are an essential link in the nutritional cycle of animals and crops.

The book became a huge success – it was reprinted nine times – and prompted an enormously enthusiastic international response. The *Times Literary Supplement* described it as 'more than an exposition of doctrine, it is a demand for the recognition of the importance of the biological fact in soil fertility'. The newly nicknamed 'Compost Queen' had spoken – and was heard.

Throughout her life, Eve Balfour always maintained she had not set out to form any sort of movement. But she, of all people, should have known what grows from little acorns. ... After the publication of *The Living Soil*, she received letters from all over the world, urging her to set up some kind of international forum in the furtherance of her ideas. Subsequently, in 1946, the Soil Association was formed, partly to support the research at Haughley and also to campaign worldwide for a more holistic approach to farming and nutrition. As well as managing the research farm, Eve served as the Association's General Secretary for many years.

In the first issue of *Mother Earth*, the Association's magazine, in 1946, Eve set out its *raison d'être*:

> The Soil Association, armed with real knowledge and the ability to interpret it, must use it to educate public opinion, not only regarding the need for a healthy soil – the source of our food – but also concerning the way in which that food should or should not be treated once it is grown.[17]

Its first general meeting approved its objectives, which have since never been revised, although in recent years the Association has placed more emphasis on campaigning rather than pure research:

1. To bring together all those working for a fuller understanding of the relationship between soil, plant, animal and man;

2. To initiate, co-ordinate and assist research in the field; and

3. To collect and distribute the knowledge gained so as to create a body of informed opinion.

By 1952 the Soil Association had 3,000 members in forty-two different countries. However, Haughley and Eve Balfour were sneered at by the scientific establishment; she was dismissed as a 'mystic' – only just short of the old smear reserved for women: 'witch'. One scientist who did support the project was Dr Victor Stewart, who later recalled, 'To admit to knowing Lady Eve and respecting her views was not the best way for an agricultural scientist to seek professional preferment.'[18] It is safe to assume that, had Haughley been set up and run by a team of academically qualified men, it would have been considered eminently more credible and noteworthy by the government and the agricultural establishment.

During the 1950s, with the growth of the Association's international reputation, Eve embarked on a number of foreign tours to exchange information and knowledge on organic farming techniques. In 1951, she visited America. During her six-week stay, she managed to cram in eighteen lectures, fifteen radio broadcasts and numerous interviews.

Two years later, she returned to America and embarked on an exploratory tour, financed along the way by lectures, and described later as '9,600 Miles in a Station Wagon'. Accompanying Eve on this tour was her partner, Kathleen Carnley, with whom she lived in a cottage at Haughley after the large farmhouse was rented out. Kathleen, known to everyone as 'KC', had joined the Haughley set during the 1930s, as a particularly skilful dairy worker.

Eve and KC's 9,600 miles began in Lancaster, Pennsylvania, and took in eleven states in three months. Eve did the driving, while KC took care of the arrangements for the busy schedule of lectures and meetings. They also visited organic farms and gardens and met with agricultural scientists, ecologists and businessmen to discuss the possible formation of an Ecological Research Foundation. Although she was impressed with the efforts of many of the professionals she met to challenge the conventional approach to food and health, Eve concluded:

> The vested interests in ill-health, and products which cause it, have a vice-like grip over everybody and everything. The population is very diet-conscious but only a small minority

is informed. The majority imagine they can keep well by consuming vast quantities of synthetic vitamin pills.[19]

In November 1958, she and KC left England for a year-long visit to Australia and New Zealand. There, they were particularly impressed by the use of Keypoint farm dams for water conservation and irrigation. They visited a 40,000-acre sheep-station in Western Queensland, where they learned about the perils of kangaroo ticks and enjoyed the numerous parrots and kookaburras. In Brisbane they saw toads the size of hedgehogs, originally imported to devour insects on the sugar-cane plantations. At Bundaberg, they were shown how the cane, usually a heavily fertilized crop, could be grown organically. In Tasmania, they met the first Australian members of the Soil Association. Also on this trip, they were introduced to the surprising Antipodean custom of leaving bathroom and toilet doors unlocked – even in hotels, the doors had no locks. Eve later mused, 'I never met an Australian who could tell me the reason for this custom.'[20]

Before their return to England, Eve made a radio broadcast in Perth, in which she urged Australians to preserve the unspoilt areas of bushland and to carry out more research into water conservation. She also reminded the urban dwellers to have more regard for their rural neighbours: 'Never forget that your prosperity and industrial expansion depend on the prosperity of the country.'[21]

In 1961, Eve bought a cottage in Theberton, Suffolk, for £350 and she and KC moved in. This was to be their home for the rest of their lives. The 1970s brought them an even share of welcome developments and bitter disappointments.

For years, the Soil Association, together with the Pye Trust, had struggled to continue financing the project at Haughley. The problems had been exacerbated by a split in the Association's members over what priority a seemingly expensive research project should be given. In 1970, the thirty-year-old experiment was put out to pasture. On a happier note, in 1975, a new edition of *The Living Soil* was published, together with a full report on the results of the Haughley Experiment.

Despite her increasing differences with the Association over policy, Eve continued to give lectures, attend conferences and present papers wherever possible – she did not officially retire until 1984. In 1977, she and Mary Langman drove across France, stopping off to visit various farms along the way. Their ultimate destination was a conference organized by the International Federation of Organic Agricultural Movements at Sissach in Switzerland, where Eve presented a paper, eventually published in pamphlet form.

At ninety, Eve Balfour was living at Theberton alone: after fifty years together, KC had died. Despite a home help once a fortnight and some assistance with the gardening, Eve was still resolutely independent, growing all her own vegetables and making her own bread. Her holistic approach to her own health and diet incorporated vegetarianism, wholefood – and the odd indulgence. She warned one enquiring soul not to model themselves on her: 'I drink gin and tonic and smoke cigarettes. As long as you're good 75 per cent of the time, the remaining 25 per cent will look after itself.'

And she still generated press interest: she was the subject of a programme for Anglia Television's *Farming Diary* series and, the year before she died, *Country Living* ran an excellent article about her, which was at once revealing and heaving with euphemisms. Eve's hair, we were told, was cut 'in an elongated Eton cut, the style favoured by so many early career women'. She had worn trousers since the First World War when 'she discovered the freedom of breeches' and 'very sensibly she chooses men's slippers for comfort'. After discovering her preference for sensible shoes, it will come as no surprise, then, to learn that 'she was never seriously interested in marriage or children and is content now to live alone since the death of her close friend of 50 years'.

Not long after this interview, she suffered a stroke from which she never fully recovered. She was awarded the OBE in the New Year's Honours, announced shortly before she died on 15 January 1990, at the age of ninety-one – the very same day that the government announced it was to give the first-ever funding to organic farming. If Eve heard about this before she died, it must have given her a good laugh – after all, it had only taken fifty years.

In May 1991, a memorial service for her was held at Marylebone Parish Church in London. The speakers included Mary Langman of the Wholefood Trust; Patrick Holden, Director of the

British Organic Farmers' and Organic Growers' Association and, incongruously, John Selwyn Gummer, then Minister of Agriculture, Fisheries and Food – the man who, in the middle of a health scare about 'mad cow disease', made his small daughter eat a hamburger in front of the press to prove that the distinctly non-organically produced British beef was perfectly safe.

Reflecting on Eve Balfour's contribution, Mary Langman wrote, 'I do not think that she herself will come to be seen as one of the great originators, but rather as one who worked continuously and with the most acute perception to bring together insights derived from different fields.'[22] Perhaps it was her early supporter, Victor Stewart, who summed up her life and work best when, after her death, he observed, 'She kept alive the idea that there is an alternative.'

Notes

1. *Listener*, 25 October 1956.
2. *Ibid.*
3. Elizabeth Lutyens, *A Goldfish Bowl* (London, Cassell, 1972), p. 8.
4. Wilfred Cooper, *Land Girl* (London, English Universities Press, 1941), p. 12.
5. M. and S. Harries, *A Pilgrim Soul* (London, Michael Joseph, 1989), p. 61.
6. Lutyens, *Goldfish Bowl*, p. 8.
7. Letter to the author, 3 August 1993.
8. *Listener*, 25 October 1956.
9. *The Times*, 3 August 1933.
10. *Ibid.*, 8 July.
11. *Ibid.*, 3 August.
12. Ethel Smyth, *Female Pipings in Eden* (London, Peter Davies, 1933), p. 189.
13. *The Times*, 4 April 1934.
14. *Ibid.*, 12 January 1935.
15. *Living Earth*, April/June 1990, p. 8.
16. E. B. Balfour, *The Living Soil and the Haughley Experiment* (New York, Universe Books, 1943), introduction.
17. Nigel Dudley, *The Soil Association Handbook* (London, Macdonald Optima, 1991, p. 3.
18. *Living Earth*, April/June 1990, p. 8.
19. *Mother Earth*, September 1951, p. 13.

20.   *Ibid.*, October 1961, p. 45.
21.   *Ibid.*, p. 55.
22.   *Living Earth*, April/June 1990, p. 4.

Maureen Colquhoun

SIR Ian McKellen has ruffled some feathers since he came out in 1988: he has come in for criticism over his acceptance of a knighthood and his subsequent meeting with Prime Minister John Major to discuss lesbian and gay rights. But, whatever the rights and wrongs of these actions, he probably caused more anger and offence when, in 1992, he told the London paper *Capital Gay* that, before he came out, there was no one else in public life who had taken such a step: 'I had no example. There was nobody in British life, full stop, who'd come out. ... Maybe Derek Jarman ... but no gay politician, no gay actors.' Jarman found it insulting: 'It's a rewriting of our history. ... To say there was nobody out in British life is crazy, outrageous.' Yes, all of that. And patently incorrect, to boot. Perhaps McKellen was unaware that, prior to his formation of the by-invitation-only lobbying organization, the Stonewall Group, there had been an out lesbian MP who could have done with more support and honesty from other prominent gay people ten years before his positive step.

Maureen Colquhoun was born in the sedate seaside town of Eastbourne, Sussex, in August 1928 and brought up in a socialist one-parent family. She joined the Labour Party herself in 1945 and went on to take a degree in economics at the London School of Economics. In 1949, she married the novelist and journalist Keith Colquhoun, and they had a daughter and two sons.

From 1965 until 1974, she was a member of Shoreham District Council, Adur District Council and West Sussex County Council. She unsuccessfully stood as Labour candidate for

Tonbridge in the 1970 general election. At the next, in February 1974, she won the new constituency of Northampton North with a majority of 1033. Eight months later, she regained the seat with the slightly increased majority of 1538. At that time, there were only twenty-eight women MPs in Britain and Colquhoun was disappointed at what she saw as a distinct lack of feminism in the House. 'There were some near-miss feminists among the Labour women,' she said. 'There was no willingness to dismantle the patriarchal society because many of them hadn't heard of it!'[1]

She settled down to parliamentary life, with all its rules, rituals and disappointments. On her first day in the House, she was queuing up for lunch in the members' cafeteria when her good friend, Arthur Blenkinsop, MP for South Shields, said how good it was that she was an MP at last. He looked at his tray of food and said to her, 'And now you're here, you've got to do something about the quality of this food.' 'You deal with the bloody food,' said the new member for Northampton North, 'I'm going to be Chancellor of the Exchequer.'[2]

The carved-in-granite left-wing MP, Dennis Skinner, showed her the ropes, teaching her how to table parliamentary questions and early day motions (formal expressions of opinion open to other MPs to sign). She caused a stir with one such motion, which stated, 'That recognising the destruction to family life of Honourable Members caused by the uncivilised working hours in the House, this House resolves that it shall sit on five days a week between the hours of 9 a.m. and 6 p.m.' This soon found itself amended – as was the way with early day motions – to read, 'that a truly democratic House of Commons cannot be run on an office hours timetable; and that those who cannot stand the heat should get out of, or back to, the kitchen'.[3] The enlightened soul who delivered this harsh lesson in parliamentary trickery was Willie Hamilton MP. As well as women's rights, Colquhoun took a keen interest in the problems of Northern Ireland and was a sponsor of the Legalize Cannabis Campaign.

In May 1975, she presented a Private Member's Bill to Parliament, the Balance of Sexes Bill. At that time there were no women on such bodies as the Post Office Board, the Electricity Council, the National Bus Company or the Civil Aviation Authority. The Arts Council of Great Britain constituted three women and seventeen men. In the House of Lords, out of 1,105 nobles and clergy, there were a mere fifty women. Colquhoun's bill, if passed, would have ensured equal representation on all these bodies. But, like so many contentious or radical Private Members' Bills, it did not become law. It was, however, to set off the sequence of events which would change her life, both personally and politically.

One of those who took a keen interest in the bill was Barbara Todd, drama adviser at the British Council, feminist, founder of the lesbian magazine *Sappho*, and mother of two teenage daughters. She had been commissioned to write a feature about the bill for *Nova* magazine. She wrote to Colquhoun and they arranged to have tea at the Commons, together with Dr Una Kroll, deaconess of the Church of England.

But it was not, apparently, love at first sight. According to Colquhoun, 'Babs told me at our first meeting she thought I was a typical poorly dressed Labour woman MP with a good idea for women in the bill I was promoting.'[4] However, during the weeks of campaigning on the Sex Discrimination Bill and abortion amendment bills, they grew closer. As Colquhoun described it, 'By the time the House met to debate the second reading of the Balance of Sexes Bill, I knew that Babs loved me and she knew that I loved her.'[5] In the public gallery, sitting side by side but unaware of who the other was, were Babs Todd and Keith Colquhoun.

Colquhoun said later she had known for some years that she preferred women but kept it to herself while her children were growing up, not wishing them to be brought up in a one-parent family. In an interview in the *Sunday Times* in 1980 Colquhoun admitted, 'Falling in love with Babs was the last thing I wanted.' But the 'last thing' had happened and Colquhoun knew that she could keep up the pretence no longer. She came out to her own family and went to live with Babs Todd and her daughters.

In 1978 she gave an interview to *Woman's Own* magazine (later quoted in *Gay News*), which was headlined, 'It's Marvellous to Be in Love Again'. As well as praising her ex-husband and her children for their support, she spoke of her love for Babs: 'I just took off into the orbit of love and nothing else mattered. I still liken it to being in love for the first time; it's almost like being 20 again.'[6]

The story had been broken by the *Daily Mail* in 1976 in Nigel Dempster's gossip column. That spring, the new Colquhoun–Todd household had sent out invitations to friends for a joint house-warming and birthday party. The invitations featured a cartoon illustration of the double-women's sign, with Todd smoking a cigarette and Colquhoun, as she put it, 'looking smug'.

Soon it emerged that members of the press were making enquiries among Colquhoun's friends and constituents. Keith Colquhoun was telephoned by Nigel Dempster, asking him to comment on 'the break-up of your marriage'. Other members of the 'Diary' team telephoned the Colquhoun–Todd home relentlessly and approached *Sappho* and the British Council for a photograph of Babs. After the story appeared on 15 April, their house was besieged by reporters and photographers, as was the home of Colquhoun's seventy-eight-year-old mother. The bell rang endlessly, while photographers with telephoto lenses hid in bushes, desperate to get a snap of them. When Colquhoun subsequently complained to the Press Council about this intolerable invasion of privacy, they upheld the conduct of the *Daily Mail* reporters.

Three years later, Colquhoun and Todd discovered how Dempster got the story. One of the guests invited to the party was a school teacher, who was about to start work in America. One of her female colleagues was married to a journalist who, one night, 'doorstepped' the teacher and threatened to tell the American Embassy in London that she was a lesbian if she did not spill the beans about Colquhoun. This would almost certainly have resulted in her visa application being turned down 'for reasons of deviancy'.

At the time of the Dempster story, Colquhoun was dismayed at the reactions from those in her own party. Most would never discuss the subject; those who did were hostile. One Labour woman MP, the late Millie Miller, complained to her, 'Now we [women MPs] won't be able to have our hair short or wear trousers in public for fear of being labelled ... lesbian!'[7] And this, as Colquhoun observed, from a heterosexual grandmother with very short hair and a baggy trouser suit to a lesbian grandmother with long hair, wearing a skirt, a silk blouse and high-heeled shoes.

In the meantime, Colquhoun's constituents and local party seemed more accepting. When she attended constituency events and campaigned for Labour in local elections, Babs Todd accompanied her as her partner. Colquhoun even changed her entry in *Who's Who*: from 1975, Babs was listed as her partner. But it was merely the quiet before the storm.

Labour Party expert, David Butler, said in 1978 that personal considerations – 'drink, divorce or neglect of constituency business' – were responsible for most MP–Constituency Labour Party battles.[8] But Maureen Colquhoun's case was to fall outside these parameters.

In January 1977, Enoch Powell made another of his inflammatory remarks about immigration, this time prophesying civil war. He came under attack from all directions, including a complaint from Winston Churchill, Tory MP for Stretford: 'Far from warning of the dangers of large-scale immigration to Britain at a time when the problem could have been avoided, Mr Powell was part of the political generation responsible for that immigration.'[9]

Colquhoun was at a women's rights seminar in Norwich when she was telephoned by Chris Moncrieff, a journalist seeking Labour Party reactions to Powell's remarks. According to Colquhoun, she had become disillusioned with the Labour government's handling of racism and let off steam to Moncrieff on the subject. 'The real bogymen', she said, 'are in the Labour Party, who use soft words and put no money into solving the problems of poor blacks and poor whites in inner cities.'[10] 'It is increasingly difficult to talk intelligently about the race issue within the Labour Party. They prefer to attack Powell rather than attack the real problems of racial conflict,' she added.[11] In this case, they also preferred to attack Colquhoun. Bashir Mann, deputy chair of the Commission for Racial Equality, sent a telegram to the Tribune Group, complaining about Colquhoun's comments. Her constituency party also asked her to explain her views to them – something she was happy to do. They withdrew their complaints and accepted her explanation, as did the Northampton Race Relations Council AGM.

By a strange coincidence, in 1993, black Labour MP Bernie Grant called on the government to help black Britons who wanted to take advantage of 'voluntary repatriation', at a fringe meeting of the Labour Party conference. It was a view regarded as out of line with many in his own party and groups such as the Anti-Racist Alliance but which underlined the despair felt by so many black people about the combination of old and new racism, and the inability of the main political parties to tackle the problem effectively. The only politician to support Grant's views was – Winston Churchill, MP for Davyhulme.

Given Colquhoun's general political make-up, it is ludicrous to think that she could ever be counted as a supporter of Enoch Powell or of any other individuals or groups with similar views. While still a local councillor in Shoreham, she was thrown off all her council committees for advocating that the council allocate 10 per cent of new council houses to immigrant families. If she made a mistake over the Powell incident, it is perhaps that she said the right thing at the wrong time, for it was certainly true that at the time the Labour Party shied away from tackling racism, and anyone who raised the issue was not popular.

However, the incident seemed to be the opportunity Colquhoun's constituency party enemies had been waiting for and they seized it with gusto. In March 1977, a motion was put forward to the 62-strong General Management Committee, under the auspices of the Young Socialists. It read:

> This GMC feels that, in view of her recent statements and public behaviour, Mrs Colquhoun is no longer acceptable as the representative in Parliament of Northampton North constituency, and therefore states its intention not to adopt her as candidate at the next general election. We therefore resolve that she should retire and that the national executive be requested to give permission to select a new candidate.[12]

Members of other branches within the constituency were sceptical about the motives behind this move, while Colquhoun defended herself in a letter to *The Times*: 'There is no doubt that as well as being unpopular, Members of Parliament can come to grief with their own party activists for reasons that are no fault of theirs.' She revealed that a meeting with her GMC had been arranged for 2 July: 'It is then that I will know what it is all about ... I understand it is largely based on what the party saw as my support for Enoch

Powell when I said that he "might sometimes be listened to". This was taken out of context.'[13]

Norman Ashley, the GMC chair, maintained, 'Her sexual behaviour is not the issue',[14] and that the real reason involved 'a lot of small things which amounted to larger things when added up'. Some of these 'small things' were alleged to be her comment that the Duke of Edinburgh had become a 'British joke'; that she had swapped blows with a car-park attendant who, in a mix-up over parking permits, had brought down a barrier on her car and then abused her verbally; and a seemingly innocuous request that British Rail stopped stamping their season tickets 'male' and 'female'. Another delegate alleged that Colquhoun had not attended enough constituency surgeries – an allegation refuted by Colquhoun's record, which showed that, out of twenty-eight consecutive weekends, she had spent twenty-five on Labour Party and constituency work.

One correspondent, clearly not a Colquhoun fan, wrote irately to *Spare Rib*:

> Who says Maureen Colquhoun was sacked for being a lesbian? As a member of the neighbouring constituency ... in this area we are suffering from massive cuts in health expenditure, cuts in education, an inefficient Social Security system. ... What do we hear from Maureen Colquhoun? A tale about bopping a car-park attendant, stupid comments about women drivers being incompetent and the Powell statement – made just a week before we were beginning an anti-racialism campaign in Northampton![15]

Her supporters included some surprising, and encouraging, parties. Delegates from the Liberal Party conference, including a number of their most popular and prominent MPs, sent her a letter of sympathy, expressing disgust at the GMC's decision, 'apparently because you are open and honest about being a lesbian'. It stated that they regarded her treatment as 'a fundamental infringement of civil liberties', adding that 'politicians should be judged by their political performance and not by their private lives'.[16] In her book, *Women in the House*, Elizabeth Vallance said that the most

Colquhoun could be accused of was political naivety in believing 'that it was possible to publicise this [her sexuality] without some such repercussion'. However, she was convinced of the opponents' real motive: 'It seems clear that her own avowed sexual attitudes and practices were the real basis of their disapproval.'[17]

On 27 September, the GMC voted 23–18 to remove Maureen Colquhoun as Labour candidate. She appealed to the Party's National Executive Committee, and a Colquhoun Action Committee was set up, lobbying Parliament and picketing the NEC inquiry. Delegates from the National Union of Railwaymen challenged the conduct of the GMC and concluded that Colquhoun was, indeed, being persecuted because of her private life.

Eventually, the NEC upheld her appeal but, no sooner had this decision been arrived at, than her Northampton North CLP once again began proceedings to deselect her. In March 1978, members of the Park Ward branch of the local party submitted another resolution asking the CLP not to readopt her as candidate. The party's Executive Committee voted by 27–18 to consider the resolution at a special meeting – and so it began again. Colquhoun pledged to fight on, even though she was doubtful about her prospects of representing Northampton North. In the interview with *Woman's Own* magazine, she said:

> In some ways, being a lesbian has ruined my political career. I think they'll select another candidate to fight the next General Election. However, I don't intend to be beaten. If I lose their support I shall stand alone representing Human Rights.[18]

The battle dragged on acrimoniously through 1978. In April of that year, a dozen or so lesbians held a sit-in protest at the office of Derek Jameson, then editor of the *Daily Express*. The paper's much-prized gossip columnist, the late Jean Rook, had written a disparaging piece about Colquhoun, headlined, 'The Gay Lady Is a Bore', which focused entirely on her sexuality. Lesbians were Rook's prime target at this time: a few months earlier, she had written a particularly nasty article about lesbian mothers. Interestingly, Jameson himself, though defending Rook's right to freedom of expression, said he thought it 'barbarous and inhuman' to suggest that lesbians should not have children or that they should have their children taken away from them. The women managed to get Jameson to agree to run a full-page, more balanced article on Maureen, together with a comment piece by the Maureen Colquhoun Action Committee.

Meanwhile, Colquhoun was out and proud with a vengeance. She attended the national conference of the Campaign for Homosexual Equality, the leading campaign group for gay rights in the 1970s. But her speech was no pat on the back: CHE was 'as ineffective as it is possible to be,' she told delegates, it 'must become a political force, prepared to stand up and be counted if it is to continue to represent gay people'. Prophetically, she warned them that, at the next general election, lesbians and gay men would face an 'unholy alliance' between Margaret Thatcher and the reactionary 'clean-up' campaigner Mary Whitehouse. She also urged the gay movement to be vigilant during the trial of former Liberal Party leader, Jeremy Thorpe, then charged with conspiracy to murder the man alleged to be his ex-lover, Norman Scott. 'From October', she warned, 'there will be a horrifying barrage of anti-gay publicity in the press morning, noon and night – day upon day – that will rub off on us all. We must be in a position of strength.'[19]

Two months later, she tabled an early day motion in the Commons, to which fourteen other Labour MPs (including Neil Kinnock) put their names. The motion originally read:

> That this House congratulates the Mayor of Wolverhampton, and all those who supported her, in the proper and civilised decision that she took in supporting the Wolverhampton Group of CHE's [Campaign for Homosexual Equality's] right to be represented in the town's commemoration of the dead of two world wars and to lay a wreath to the memory of those homosexuals who died alongside their heterosexual countrymen.

Unfortunately, Ronald Bell, MP for Beaconsfield, tabled an amendment which read, 'Leave out from "House" to end and add "expresses its abhorrence of buggery and lesbianism and deplores the exhibitionism of those who have succumbed to these sordid perversions." [20]

But in April 1979, shortly after Prime Minister James Callaghan announced there was to be a general election in May, the Northampton North CLP dissidents backed down and the Constituency Selection Committee voted 26–17 to adopt Maureen Colquhoun as their candidate – with the full backing of Labour's NEC. The candidate herself was jubilant. She paid tribute to all those, in and out of the constituency, who had supported her: 'The hard core were ordinary people, solid working class people whom you might have expected to be prejudiced – but they weren't. That's my victory – and it's our victory too. The message for gay people is "Be out".' [21]

Unfortunately, she was denied her ultimate victory: in May 1979, Margaret Thatcher swept into power and, in the wake of the national swing to the Conservatives, Tony Marlow swept out Maureen Colquhoun. We can never be sure how much the bitter deselection row and the hostile press coverage she received contributed to this result. But it is perhaps worth pointing out that, although Northampton North was certainly a marginal seat, it is also true that all the Labour women MPs with small majorities were vulnerable in the face of the national swing to the Conservatives. Other prominent women MPs who were unseated on the crest of the Tory wave included Helene Hayman and Audrey Wise.

A year later, Colquhoun published *A Woman in the House*, her own account of her time in Parliament, her struggles in Northampton and the effects of falling in love with another woman and coming out. In an interview in the *Sunday Times* she reaffirmed her commitment to the Labour Party, saying, 'You have to work for change from inside.' She confirmed that she would be seeking adoption as a Labour candidate in a winnable seat.

But Maureen Colquhoun did not manage to get back 'inside'. In 1981, she made an unsuccessful attempt to be nominated as Labour candidate for the seat of Brecon and Radnor, which was lost to the Tories in the 1979 election. She did, however, serve on Hackney Borough Council from 1982 to 1990. She worked as an information officer for Gingerbread, the organization which supports single parents, was a trustee and Honorary Treasurer of the Albany Society for ten years and served as Honorary Secretary of the All-Party Parliamentary Group on AIDS. Two years ago, she and Babs Todd left London and set up home in the Lake District.

Labour's hard and soft Left are a shadow of their former selves. In the last decade, unsuccessful bids for the party leadership and deputy leadership have been staged by Tony Benn, the late Eric Heffer, John Prescott, Bryan Gould and Ann Clwyd. Other stalwarts of the Left, including Jo Richardson and Bob Cryer, have died recently. Those remaining, such as Bernie Grant and Ken Livingstone, have high media profiles but are largely kept at arm's length by the majority of their parliamentary colleagues, and as far away from party decision-making as possible. None of this will have come as a surprise to Colquhoun. In 1980, she spoke of the impending demise of the Labour Left, 'controlled by a right wing socialist-democratic Labour Government who respected the status quo, upheld the civil service departments and neglected their own people – working people'. She observed that, in many respects, 'There appeared to be little difference between the political thinking of the Labour establishment and the political thinking of some of our Liberal and Tory opponents.'[22] These prophetic criticisms are, of course, at the heart of the disillusionment felt by many of those who reluctantly support the 'modernized', PR- and image-conscious Labour Party.

At the time of writing, the House of Commons has a record number of women MPs – fifty-eight, up from forty-one; there were also a record number of female candidates in the 1992 general election – 548, nearly double the previous total. And, for once, Labour showed signs that it had stopped its tradition of putting most of its women candidates in unwinnable seats. But a recent attempt to raise the number of Labour women MPs by imposing short-list quotas on constituencies has been vilified by many within the party who seem quite satisfied with the snail's pace of women's progress.

In 1985, Lisanne Radice wrote a pamphlet, *Winning Women's Votes*, in which she observed that Labour's so-called 'A-list' – of union-sponsored candidates – still remained the preserve of white men. 'Trade unions need to be asked to reconsider their attitude to women candidates,' she said.[23] Some have: this has resulted in the emergence of MPs such as Clare Short and Audrey Wise. But now, as then, change is needed most among the membership of the constituency parties and for this to happen, as Radice pointed out, 'the Labour Party has to lose its image as a male-dominated party'. And Radice's observation, made about the Labour Party's attitudes to women in the mid-1980s, could doubly apply to its attitudes to gay women today: 'Whilst in theory there is an understanding that society has changed, in practice this does not apply in terms of attitudinal research, policy making or projection of propaganda.'[24] A year after she wrote this, the report, *British Social Attitudes – Homosexuality*, stated that more hostility towards lesbians and gay men was found 'among committed Labour voters than other parties'.

Chris Smith remains Britain's only openly gay MP, coming out in 1985 at a gay rights' rally in Rugby. As yet, no man or woman has stood successfully as an openly gay candidate. When Smith came out, he was already a sitting MP – albeit in a marginal seat – and did not initially have to suffer the campaign of dirty tricks, smears and intimidation endured by Peter Tatchell at the hands of the media, the Social Democrats and Labour's leadership when he stood as Labour candidate in the Bermondsey by-election of February 1983.

In 1993, the actor and Stonewall founder Michael Cashman made an unsuccessful attempt to be adopted as a Labour candidate for a European parliamentary seat. Two out lesbians have served as local council leaders in London: Anne Matthews in Southwark and Linda Bellos in neighbouring Lambeth. But no other British MP has felt able to emulate Chris Smith's example – and this, despite the fact that, far from losing his seat and his standing in the party, he is currently Labour spokesperson on environmental issues. Furthermore, after notices placed in the gay press, lesbians and gay men flocked to his Islington South and Finsbury constituency to volunteer their services during the 1992 general election. His constituency record and their efforts combined to turn his slender majority of less than a thousand votes into a thumping 10,652.

The front and back benches on both sides of the Commons

are dotted with closeted gay men and women, some of them preferring to hide behind artificial marriages. It is common knowledge around Parliament, and in the grass roots of the lesbian and gay community, who most of them are but, with typical British politeness, the tactic of 'outing' has not caught on in this country, unlike the way that American activists, sick of the hypocrisy and betrayals, have used it to smash the glass houses of closeted American politicians and public figures.

Meanwhile, John Major's government has continued to deny equality to gay men, in the recent (February 1994) vote that reduced their age of consent only to eighteen. As for the Labour Party, it seems as depressingly confused and ambivalent on lesbian and gay rights as ever. In 1987, the front bench made a complete hash of its handling of Section 28 – a depressing number of Labour MPs actually supported the damn thing when it was first unveiled. Alice Mahon, MP for Halifax, told *Gay Life* magazine in 1988, 'I was ashamed of our front bench. I was absolutely appalled.'

On paper, Labour's policy, as passed at the 1985 annual conference and subsequently reaffirmed, is for full equality for lesbians and gay men, including equalizing the age of consent and repealing all discriminatory sections of the law, including Section 28. But ... even this commitment, at the time of writing, goes with a proviso that it would come about by way of a private member's bill. Shadow Home Secretary Tony Blair has called on his party colleagues to support an equal age of consent, but the issue would still come down to a free vote. Early in 1994, in a shameful episode, the Shadow Education Secretary, Ann Taylor, and Shadow Health Secretary, David Blunkett, both voted against Edwina Currie's Criminal Justice Bill amendment for an equal age of consent at sixteen. The late party leader John Smith backed a commitment to repealing Section 28 and the end of anti-gay discrimination in the armed forces. But deputy leader Margaret Beckett has admitted to having reservations about lesbian or gay couples being allowed to foster children – a view not made public until after individual members of the Labour Party had cast their votes in the deputy leadership contest.

An exasperated correspondent to the letters page of the *Pink Paper* asked, 'Does the Labour Party really expect us to look to

Edwina Currie as the only champion of the fight for all our rights in Parliament?'[25]

As recently as December 1993, former leader Neil Kinnock revealed to a Young Labour Party meeting that he had 'personally resisted' Labour adopting a pledge for an equal age of consent as party policy during his time in office, and that although he backed some sort of reduction he was 'not sure' that it ought to be lowered to sixteen. This virtually answered all the questions about the Labour leadership's 'hands-off' attitude towards lesbian and gay rights for a decade.

In America, President Clinton and his former Defense Secretary, Les Aspin, made a pig's ear over the pledge to end the ban on gays in the military. But at least the Clinton administration and inner circle boasts a healthy number of out lesbian and gay appointees, including San Francisco councillor Roberta Achtenberg, Assistant Secretary for Fair Housing and Equal Opportunities at the Department of Housing and Urban Development.

In this country, there is a fundamental, deep-rooted problem which the Labour Party has to address: why is it acceptable for Chris Smith to be an MP and Michael Cashman to apply to be a candidate when, in the 1980s and 1990s, the nearest our lesbians get to political office is as unsalaried leaders of councils? Perhaps the truth lies in an observation made by Elizabeth Vallance: 'It is still the case that the standards, personal as well as public, which are demanded of women are rather different from those expected of a man.'[26]

The essence of the political visibility and acceptability of lesbians in Britain was captured brilliantly by cartoonist David Shenton in a typically witty and astute strip. A gay man finds one of his lesbian friends in floods of tears. He wants to know what is wrong. She wails, 'I'm a lesbian ... and a socialist ... *and I don't have anybody to vote for!*'

Notes

1.   Maureen Colquhoun, *A Woman in the House* (Shoreham-by-Sea, Scan Books, 1980), p. 11.
2.   *Ibid.*, p. 45.

3. *Ibid.*, pp. 13–14.
4. *Ibid.*, p. 66.
5. *Ibid.*, p. 67.
6. *Gay News*, 21 September 1978.
7. Colquhoun, *Woman in the House*, p. 92.
8. Alison Young, *The Reselection of MPs* (London, Heinemann, 1983), p. 100.
9. *The Times*, 24 January 1977.
10. Colquhoun, *Woman in the House*, p. 55.
11. *The Times*, 22 August 1977.
12. *Ibid.*
13. *Ibid.*, 4 May.
14. *Ibid.*, 29 September.
15. *Spare Rib*, December 1977.
16. *The Times*, 1 October 1977.
17. Elizabeth Vallance, *Women in the House: Study of Women MPs* (London, The Athlone Press, 1982), p. 203.
18. Quoted in *Gay News*, 21 September 1978.
19. *Gay News*, 7 September.
20. *Ibid.*, 30 November.
21. *Ibid.*, 19 April 1979.
22. Colquhoun, *Woman in the House*, p. 50.
23. Lisanne Radice, *Winning Women's Votes* (London, Fabian Society, 1985), p. 18.
24. *Ibid.*, p. 8.
25. *Pink Paper*, 17 December 1993.
26. Vallance, *Women in the House*, p. 174.

Selected Bibliography

Adlard, Eleanor (ed.), *Edy: Recollections of Edith Craig*. London, Frederick Muller, 1949.

Ashton, Dore and Denise Browne Hare, *Rosa Bonheur: A Life and a Legend*. London, Secker and Warburg, 1981.

Bach, Steven, *Marlene Dietrich: Life and Legend*. London, Harper Collins, 1992.

Bachman, D. G. and S. Pilard, *Women Artists*. London, Methuen, 1978.

Bailey, Derrick, *Homosexuality and the Western Christian Tradition*. London, Longmans, 1955.

Baker, Michael, *Our Three Selves*. London, Hamish Hamilton, 1985.

Balfour, E. B., *The Living Soil and the Haughley Experiment*. New York, Universe Books, 1975.

Balfour, Hearnden, *The Paperchase*. London, Hodder & Stoughton, 1927.

Balfour, Hearnden, *The Enterprising Burglar*. London, Hodder & Stoughton, 1928.

Balfour, Hearnden, *Anything Might Happen*. London, Hodder & Stoughton, 1931.

Beaton, Cecil, *Diaries 1944–48*. London, Weidenfeld & Nicolson, 1972.

Beaton, Cecil, *Diaries 1955–63*. London, Weidenfeld & Nicolson, 1976.

Bell, Quentin, *Virginia Woolf*. London, Hogarth Press, 1972.

Berendsohn, Walter A., *Selma Lagerlöf: Her Life and Work*. London, Nicholson & Watson, 1931.

Boswell, John, *Rediscovering Gay History*. London, Gay Christian Movement, 1982.

Bradshaw, Jon, *Dreams That Money Can Buy*. London, Cape, 1985.

Bremer, Jan (ed.), *From Sappho to De Sade*. London, Routledge, 1989.

Brown, Judith C., *Immodest Acts: Life of a Lesbian Nun in Renaissance Italy*. Oxford, Oxford University Press, 1986.

Bryan, Benjamin, *The Vivisectors' Directory*. London, Victoria Street Society, 1884.

Burns, Edward (ed.), *Staying on Alone: Letters of Alice B. Toklas*. New York, Vintage, 1975.

Caire, Barbara, *Victorian Feminists*. Oxford, Oxford University Press, 1992.

Chappell, Jennie, *Women of Worth*. London, S. W. Partridge & Co., 1908.

Churchill, Sir Winston, *Marlborough, His Life and Times*, 2 vols. London, George Harrap, 1947.

Clark, Sir George, *The Later Stuarts 1660–1714*. Oxford, Clarendon Press, 1956.

Clement, Clara Erskine, *Women in the Fine Arts*. Boston, Houghton Mifflin, 1904.

Cobbe, Frances Power, *Broken Lights*. London, Trubner and Co., 1864.

Cobbe, Frances Power, *The Hopes of the Human Race*. London, Williams and Norgate, 1874.

Cobbe, Frances Power, *The Duties of Women*. London, Williams and Norgate, 1881.

Cobbe, Frances Power, *Life of Frances Power Cobbe*. London, Swan, Sonnenschein, 1904.

Collis, Louise, *Impetuous Heart*. London, William Kimber, 1984.

Colquhoun, Maureen, *A Woman in the House*. London, Scan Books, 1980.

Cooper, Wilfred, *Land Girl*. London, English Universities Press, 1941.

Coward, Noël, *Present Indicative*. London, Heinemann, 1937.

Crawford, Anne, *The Europa Biographical Dictionary of British Women*. London, Europa Publications, 1983.

Crichton, Ronald, *The Memoirs of Ethel Smyth* (abridged). London, Viking, 1987.

Curtis Brown, Beatrice, *The Letters of Queen Anne*. London, Cassell, 1935.

De Acosta, Mercedes, *Streets and Shadows*. New York, Longmans, 1922.

De Acosta, Mercedes, *Until the Day Break*. New York, Longmans, 1928.

De Acosta, Mercedes, *Here Lies the Heart*. London, André Deutsch, 1960.

Dudley, Nigel, *The Soil Association Handbook*. London, MacDonald Optima, 1991.

Elliman, Michael and Frederick Roll, *The Pink Plaque Guide to London*. London, GMP, 1986.

Faderman, Lillian, *Surpassing the Love of Men*. London, The Women's Press, 1985.

Fleming, Kate, *The Churchills*. London, Weidenfeld & Nicolson, 1975.

Fowler, Marian, *Blenheim*. London, Viking, 1989.

Fraser, Antonia (ed.), *Lives of the Kings and Queens of England*. London, Book Club Associates, 1975.

Gielgud, John, *Early Stages*. London, Falcon Press, 1948.

Gerrish Nunn, Pamela, *Victorian Women Artists*. London, The Women's Press, 1987.

Glendinning, Victoria, *Vita*. London, Weidenfeld & Nicolson, 1983.

Goodich, Michael, *The Unmentionable Vice*. New York, Dorset Press, 1979.

Green, David, *Sarah, Duchess of Marlborough*. London, Collins, 1967.

Green, David, *Queen Anne*. London, Collins, 1970.

Greer, Germaine, *The Obstacle Race: Fortunes of Women Painters*. London, Secker and Warburg, 1979.

Gregg, Edward, *Queen Anne*. London, Ark, 1984.

Greif, Martin, *The Gay Book of Days*. London, Comet, 1985.

Grier, Barbara, *The Lesbian in Literature*. Tallahassee, Fla., The Naiad Press, 1981.

Gronowicz, Antoni, *Garbo: Her Story*. Simon & Schuster, 1990.

Gustefson, Alrik, *Six Scandinavian Novelists*. Minneapolis, University of Minnesota Press, 1940.

Hamilton, Ian, *Writers in Hollywood*. London, Heinemann, 1990.

Harries, M. and S., *A Pilgrim Soul*. London, Joseph, 1989.

Hauser, Richard, *The Homosexual Society*. London, Bodley Head, 1962.

Higham, Charles, *Marlene*. London, Granada, 1978.

Hill, Bridget, *Eighteenth Century Women*. London, George Allen & Unwin, 1984.

Holborn, Hajo, *A History of Modern Germany 1648–1840*. London, Eyre & Spottiswoode, 1980.

Kenyon, J. P., *Stuart England*. Harmondsworth, Pelican, 1978.

Klumpke, Anna Elizabeth, *Memoirs of an Artist*. 1908.

Kristiansen, Marius, *Selma Lagerlöf*. H. A. Larsen, 1936.

Lagerlöf, Selma, *Miracles of Antichrist* (tr. P. B. Flach). Gay and Bird, 1899.

Lagerlöf, Selma, *From a Swedish Homestead* (tr. Jessie Brockmer). London, Heinemann, 1901.

Lagerlöf, Selma, 'Home and State'. London, International Women's Suffrage Alliance, 1913.

Lagerlöf, Selma, *Herr Arne's Hoard* (tr. A. G. Chater). New York, Gyldenhall, 1923.

Lagerlöf, Selma, *Memories of My Childhood* (tr. Velma Swanston Howard). Doubleday, 1934.

Lagerlöf, Selma, *The Diary of Selma Lagerlöf* (tr. Velma Swanston Howard). T. Werner Laurie, 1937.

Lahert, Richard, *Hurrah for Carrickshock!* 1986.

Leff, Gordon, *Heresy in the Middle Ages 1250–1450*. Manchester, Manchester University Press, 1967.

Legget, Jane, *Local Heroines*. London, Pandora, 1988.

Lesbian History Group, *Not a Passing Phase*. London, The Women's Press, 1989.

Lewis, Jane (ed.), *Before the Vote Was Won*. London, Routledge & Kegan Paul, 1987.

Licata, Salvatore J. and Robert P. Paterson (eds), *The Gay Past*. New York, Harrington Park Press, 1981.

Longford, Elizabeth (ed.), *Oxford Book of Royal Anecdotes*. Oxford, Oxford University Press, 1989.

Lovelance, Richard F., *Homosexuality and the Church*. London, Lamp Press, 1979.

Lutyens, Elizabeth, *A Goldfish Bowl*. London, Cassell, 1972.

Manton, Jo, *Mary Carpenter and the Children of the Streets*. London, Heinemann, 1976.

Melville, Joy, *Ellen and Edy*. London, Pandora, 1987.

Munsterberg, Hugo, *A History of Women Artists*. New York, Clarkson N. Potter, 1975.

Murphy, Kate, *Firsts: British Women Achievers*. London, The Women's Press, 1990.

Napley, Sir David, *Rasputin in Hollywood*. London, Weidenfeld & Nicolson, 1990.

Nicolson, Nigel (ed.), *Vita and Harold*. London, Weidenfeld & Nicolson, 1992.

Petersen, Karen and J. J. Wilson, *Women Artists*. London, The Women's Press, 1978.

Radice, Lisanne, *Winning Women's Votes*. London, Fabian Society, 1985.

Richards, Dell, *Lesbian Lists*. Boston, Alyson, 1990.

Riva, Maria, *Marlene Dietrich*. London, Bloomsbury, 1992.

Rowse, A. L., *The Early Churchills*. London, Macmillan, 1956.

St John, Christopher, *Hungerheart*. London, Methuen, 1915.

St John, Christopher, *Ethel Smyth: A Biography*. London, Longmans, 1959.

Scott Stevenson, R., *Famous Illnesses in History*. London, Eyre & Spottiswoode, 1962.

Sinden, Donald, *Laughter in the Second Act*. London, Hodder & Stoughton, 1985.

Smith, Don, *Early Christianity and the Homosexual*. London, Quantum Jump Press, 1979.

Smith, Edward Percy, *Remember Ellen Terry and Edith Craig*. London, English Theatre Guild, 1948.

Smyth, Ethel, *Impressions That Remained* (2 vols). London, Longmans, 1919.

Smyth, Ethel, *Streaks of Life*. London, Longmans, 1921.

Smyth, Ethel, *A Final Burning of Boats*. London, Longmans, 1928.

Smyth, Ethel, *Female Pipings in Eden*. London, Peter Davies, 1933.

Smyth, Ethel, *As Time Went On*. London, Longmans, 1936.

Smyth, Ethel, *Inordinate Affection*. London, Cresset Press, 1936.

Smyth, Ethel, *What Happened Next*. London, Longmans, 1940.

Spender, Dale, *Women of Ideas and What Men Have Done to Them*. London, Pandora Press, 1982.

Stanton, Theodore (ed.), *Reminiscences of Rosa Bonheur*. London, Andrew Melrose, 1910.

Stenton, Doris Mary, *The English Woman in History*. New York, Schocken Books, 1977.

Sturtevant, Katherine, *Our Sisters' London*. London, The Women's Press, 1991.

Terry, Ellen, *The Story of My Life*. London, Hutchinson, 1933.

Trevelyan, G. M., *England under Queen Anne*. London, Fontana, 1965.

Tufts, Eleanor, *Our Hidden Heritage: Five Centuries of Women Artists*. New York, Paddington Press, 1974.

Vallance, Elizabeth, *Women in the House: Study of Women MPs*. London, The Athlone Press, 1982.

Vickers, Hugo, *Cecil Beaton*. London, Weidenfeld & Nicolson, 1985.

de Vrieza, F. S. *Fact and Fiction in the Autobiographical Work of Selma Lagerlöf*. Assen, Van Gorum & Co., 1958.

Woolf, Virginia, *Between the Acts*. London, Hogarth Press, 1941.

Young, Alison, *The Reselection of MPs*. London, Heinemann, 1983.

Index